STUDENT

GRADE

TO

YEAR

Design by Bee & Moon
Typesetting by Racing Pigeon Productions

Graphics used in this book are derivative of various
Creative Commons works (CC0), public domain
works, or the creation of the authors. Original source
material is from *Manners, Custom and Dress During
the Middle Ages and During the Renaissance Period*, by
Paul Lacroix (1871); *The Comet of 1618 over Augsburg*
by Elias Ehinger (1573-1653]; *L'atmosphère:
Météorologie Populaire* by Camille Flammarion (1888).

http://beeandmoon.com

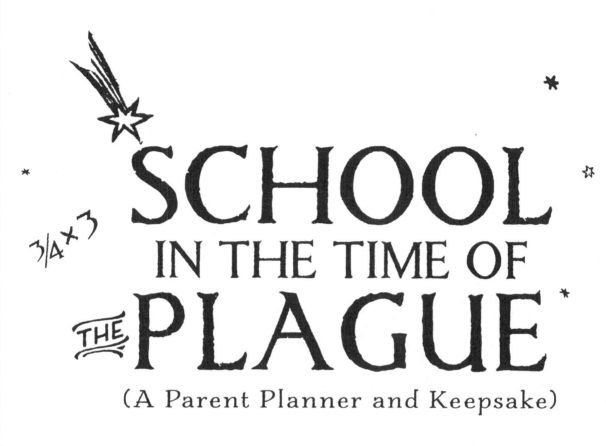

SCHOOL
IN THE TIME OF
THE PLAGUE

(A Parent Planner and Keepsake)

KATIE MACALISTER

L.K. GLOVER

How to use the weekly pages

The planner provides four pages for each academic week, providing ample room to capture necessary details.

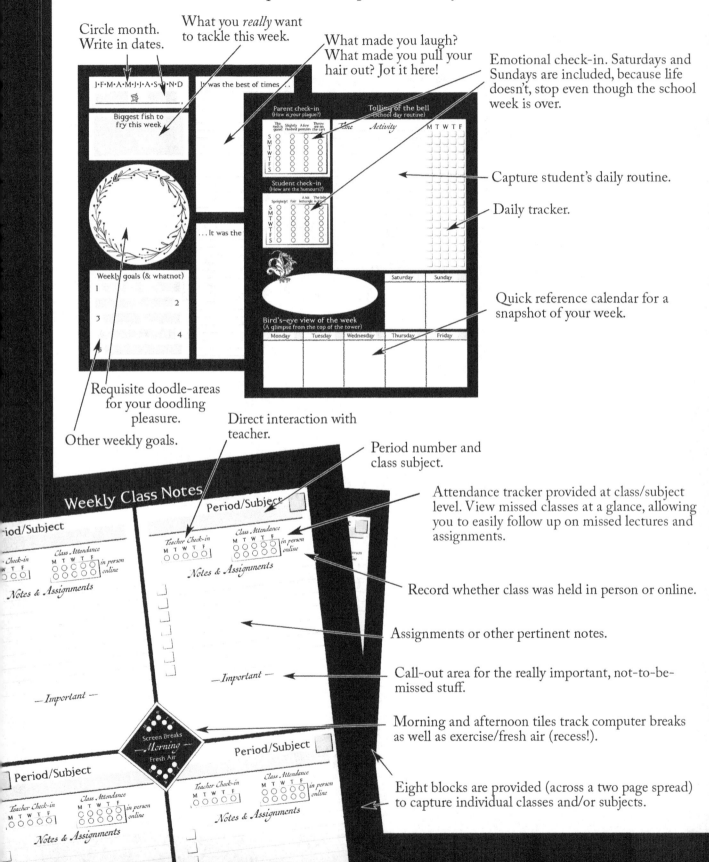

Circle month. Write in dates.

What you *really* want to tackle this week.

What made you laugh? What made you pull your hair out? Jot it here!

Emotional check-in. Saturdays and Sundays are included, because life doesn't, stop even though the school week is over.

Capture student's daily routine.

Daily tracker.

Quick reference calendar for a snapshot of your week.

Requisite doodle-areas for your doodling pleasure.

Other weekly goals.

Direct interaction with teacher.

Period number and class subject.

Attendance tracker provided at class/subject level. View missed classes at a glance, allowing you to easily follow up on missed lectures and assignments.

Record whether class was held in person or online.

Assignments or other pertinent notes.

Call-out area for the really important, not-to-be-missed stuff.

Morning and afternoon tiles track computer breaks as well as exercise/fresh air (recess!).

Eight blocks are provided (across a two page spread) to capture individual classes and/or subjects.

2020

January

Su	Mo	Tu	We	Th	Fr	Sa
			1	2	3	4
5	6	7	8	9	10	11
12	13	14	15	16	17	18
19	20	21	22	23	24	25
26	27	28	29	30	31	

February

Su	Mo	Tu	We	Th	Fr	Sa
						1
2	3	4	5	6	7	8
9	10	11	12	13	14	15
16	17	18	19	20	21	22
23	24	25	26	27	28	29

March

Su	Mo	Tu	We	Th	Fr	Sa
1	2	3	4	5	6	7
8	9	10	11	12	13	14
15	16	17	18	19	20	21
22	23	24	25	26	27	28
29	30	31				

April

Su	Mo	Tu	We	Th	Fr	Sa
			1	2	3	4
5	6	7	8	9	10	11
12	13	14	15	16	17	18
19	20	21	22	23	24	25
26	27	28	29	30		

May

Su	Mo	Tu	We	Th	Fr	Sa
					1	2
3	4	5	6	7	8	9
10	11	12	13	14	15	16
17	18	19	20	21	22	23
24	25	26	27	28	29	30
31						

June

Su	Mo	Tu	We	Th	Fr	Sa
	1	2	3	4	5	6
7	8	9	10	11	12	13
14	15	16	17	18	19	20
21	22	23	24	25	26	27
28	29	30				

July

Su	Mo	Tu	We	Th	Fr	Sa
			1	2	3	4
5	6	7	8	9	10	11
12	13	14	15	16	17	18
19	20	21	22	23	24	25
26	27	28	29	30	31	

August

Su	Mo	Tu	We	Th	Fr	Sa
						1
2	3	4	5	6	7	8
9	10	11	12	13	14	15
16	17	18	19	20	21	22
23	24	25	26	27	28	29
30	31					

September

Su	Mo	Tu	We	Th	Fr	Sa
		1	2	3	4	5
6	7	8	9	10	11	12
13	14	15	16	17	18	19
20	21	22	23	24	25	26
27	28	29	30			

October

Su	Mo	Tu	We	Th	Fr	Sa
				1	2	3
4	5	6	7	8	9	10
11	12	13	14	15	16	17
18	19	20	21	22	23	24
25	26	27	28	29	30	31

November

Su	Mo	Tu	We	Th	Fr	Sa
1	2	3	4	5	6	7
8	9	10	11	12	13	14
15	16	17	18	19	20	21
22	23	24	25	26	27	28
29	30					

December

Su	Mo	Tu	We	Th	Fr	Sa
		1	2	3	4	5
6	7	8	9	10	11	12
13	14	15	16	17	18	19
20	21	22	23	24	25	26
27	28	29	30	31		

~Important Dates~

Date	Description	Date	Description

2021

January
Su	Mo	Tu	We	Th	Fr	Sa
					1	2
3	4	5	6	7	8	9
10	11	12	13	14	15	16
17	18	19	20	21	22	23
24	25	26	27	28	29	30
31						

February
Su	Mo	Tu	We	Th	Fr	Sa
	1	2	3	4	5	6
7	8	9	10	11	12	13
14	15	16	17	18	19	20
21	22	23	24	25	26	27
28						

March
Su	Mo	Tu	We	Th	Fr	Sa
	1	2	3	4	5	6
7	8	9	10	11	12	13
14	15	16	17	18	19	20
21	22	23	24	25	26	27
28	29	30	31			

April
Su	Mo	Tu	We	Th	Fr	Sa
				1	2	3
4	5	6	7	8	9	10
11	12	13	14	15	16	17
18	19	20	21	22	23	24
25	26	27	28	29	30	

May
Su	Mo	Tu	We	Th	Fr	Sa
						1
2	3	4	5	6	7	8
9	10	11	12	13	14	15
16	17	18	19	20	21	22
23	24	25	26	27	28	29
30	31					

June
Su	Mo	Tu	We	Th	Fr	Sa
	1	2	3	4	5	
6	7	8	9	10	11	12
13	14	15	16	17	18	19
20	21	22	23	24	25	26
27	28	29	30			

July
Su	Mo	Tu	We	Th	Fr	Sa
				1	2	3
4	5	6	7	8	9	10
11	12	13	14	15	16	17
18	19	20	21	22	23	24
25	26	27	28	29	30	31

August
Su	Mo	Tu	We	Th	Fr	Sa
1	2	3	4	5	6	7
8	9	10	11	12	13	14
15	16	17	18	19	20	21
22	23	24	25	26	27	28
29	30	31				

September
Su	Mo	Tu	We	Th	Fr	Sa
			1	2	3	4
5	6	7	8	9	10	11
12	13	14	15	16	17	18
19	20	21	22	23	24	25
26	27	28	29	30		

October
Su	Mo	Tu	We	Th	Fr	Sa
					1	2
3	4	5	6	7	8	9
10	11	12	13	14	15	16
17	18	19	20	21	22	23
24	25	26	27	28	29	30
31						

November
Su	Mo	Tu	We	Th	Fr	Sa
	1	2	3	4	5	6
7	8	9	10	11	12	13
14	15	16	17	18	19	20
21	22	23	24	25	26	27
28	29	30				

December
Su	Mo	Tu	We	Th	Fr	Sa
			1	2	3	4
5	6	7	8	9	10	11
12	13	14	15	16	17	18
19	20	21	22	23	24	25
26	27	28	29	30	31	

~Important Dates~

Date	Description	Date	Description

2022

January

Su	Mo	Tu	We	Th	Fr	Sa
						1
2	3	4	5	6	7	8
9	10	11	12	13	14	15
16	17	18	19	20	21	22
23	24	25	26	27	28	29
30	31					

February

Su	Mo	Tu	We	Th	Fr	Sa
		1	2	3	4	5
6	7	8	9	10	11	12
13	14	15	16	17	18	19
20	21	22	23	24	25	26
27	28					

March

Su	Mo	Tu	We	Th	Fr	Sa
		1	2	3	4	5
6	7	8	9	10	11	12
13	14	15	16	17	18	19
20	21	22	23	24	25	26
27	28	29	30	31		

April

Su	Mo	Tu	We	Th	Fr	Sa
					1	2
3	4	5	6	7	8	9
10	11	12	13	14	15	16
17	18	19	20	21	22	23
24	25	26	27	28	29	30

May

Su	Mo	Tu	We	Th	Fr	Sa
1	2	3	4	5	6	7
8	9	10	11	12	13	14
15	16	17	18	19	20	21
22	23	24	25	26	27	28
29	30	31				

June

Su	Mo	Tu	We	Th	Fr	Sa
			1	2	3	4
5	6	7	8	9	10	11
12	13	14	15	16	17	18
19	20	21	22	23	24	25
26	27	28	29	30		

July

Su	Mo	Tu	We	Th	Fr	Sa
					1	2
3	4	5	6	7	8	9
10	11	12	13	14	15	16
17	18	19	20	21	22	23
24	25	26	27	28	29	30
31						

August

Su	Mo	Tu	We	Th	Fr	Sa
	1	2	3	4	5	6
7	8	9	10	11	12	13
14	15	16	17	18	19	20
21	22	23	24	25	26	27
28	29	30	31			

September

Su	Mo	Tu	We	Th	Fr	Sa
				1	2	3
4	5	6	7	8	9	10
11	12	13	14	15	16	17
18	19	20	21	22	23	24
25	26	27	28	29	30	

October

Su	Mo	Tu	We	Th	Fr	Sa
						1
2	3	4	5	6	7	8
9	10	11	12	13	14	15
16	17	18	19	20	21	22
23	24	25	26	27	28	29
30	31					

November

Su	Mo	Tu	We	Th	Fr	Sa
		1	2	3	4	5
6	7	8	9	10	11	12
13	14	15	16	17	18	19
20	21	22	23	24	25	26
27	28	29	30			

December

Su	Mo	Tu	We	Th	Fr	Sa
				1	2	3
4	5	6	7	8	9	10
11	12	13	14	15	16	17
18	19	20	21	22	23	24
25	26	27	28	29	30	31

~Important Dates~

Date	Description	Date	Description

AND
NOW . . .

THE
WEEKLY
PAGES

J·F·M·A·M·J·J·A·S·O·N·D

_TO_

_____ ,

Biggest fish to fry this week

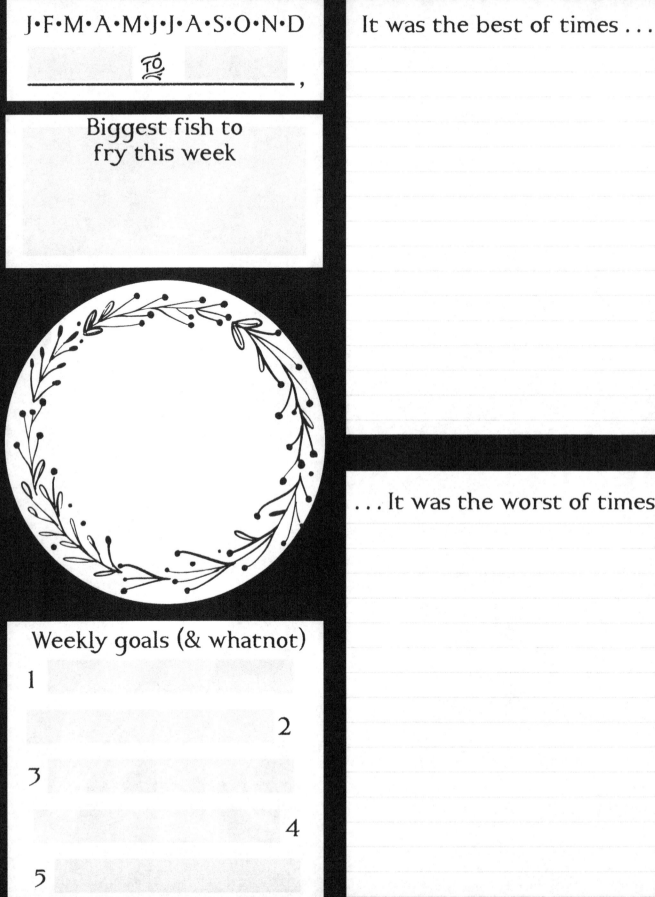

Weekly goals (& whatnot)

1

2

3

4

5

It was the best of times . . .

. . . It was the worst of times

Parent check~in
(How is your plague?)

	The rash is gone!	Slightly flushed	A few pustules	Throw me on the cart
S	○	○	○	○
M	○	○	○	○
T	○	○	○	○
W	○	○	○	○
T	○	○	○	○
F	○	○	○	○
S	○	○	○	○

Student check~in
(How are the humours?)

	Sprightly!	Fair	A bit lethargic	The bile is black
S	○	○	○	○
M	○	○	○	○
T	○	○	○	○
W	○	○	○	○
T	○	○	○	○
F	○	○	○	○
S	○	○	○	○

Tolling of the bell
(School day routine)

Time	Activity	M	T	W	T	F
		☐	☐	☐	☐	☐
		☐	☐	☐	☐	☐
		☐	☐	☐	☐	☐
		☐	☐	☐	☐	☐
		☐	☐	☐	☐	☐
		☐	☐	☐	☐	☐
		☐	☐	☐	☐	☐
		☐	☐	☐	☐	☐
		☐	☐	☐	☐	☐
		☐	☐	☐	☐	☐
		☐	☐	☐	☐	☐
		☐	☐	☐	☐	☐
		☐	☐	☐	☐	☐
		☐	☐	☐	☐	☐
		☐	☐	☐	☐	☐
		☐	☐	☐	☐	☐
		☐	☐	☐	☐	☐

Saturday	Sunday

Bird's~eye view of the week
(A glimpse from the top of the tower)

Monday	Tuesday	Wednesday	Thursday	Friday

Weekly Class Notes

Period/Subject

Teacher Check-in
M T W T F
○ ○ ○ ○ ○

Class Attendance
M T W T F
○ ○ ○ ○ ○ in person
○ ○ ○ ○ ○ online

Notes & Assignments

— Important —

Period/Subject

Teacher Check-in
M T W T F
○ ○ ○ ○ ○

Class Attendance
M T W T F
○ ○ ○ ○ ○ in person
○ ○ ○ ○ ○ online

Notes & Assignments

— Important —

Screen Breaks
Morning
Fresh Air
M T W T F
M T W T F

Period/Subject

Teacher Check-in
M T W T F
○ ○ ○ ○ ○

Class Attendance
M T W T F
○ ○ ○ ○ ○ in person
○ ○ ○ ○ ○ online

Notes & Assignments

— Important —

Period/Subject

Teacher Check-in
M T W T F
○ ○ ○ ○ ○

Class Attendance
M T W T F
○ ○ ○ ○ ○ in person
○ ○ ○ ○ ○ online

Notes & Assignments

— Important —

Weekly Class Notes

Period/Subject

Teacher Check-in
M T W T F
○ ○ ○ ○ ○

Class Attendance
M T W T F
○ ○ ○ ○ ○ *in person*
○ ○ ○ ○ ○ *online*

Notes & Assignments

— *Important* —

Period/Subject

Teacher Check-in
M T W T F
○ ○ ○ ○ ○

Class Attendance
M T W T F
○ ○ ○ ○ ○ *in person*
○ ○ ○ ○ ○ *online*

Notes & Assignments

— *Important* —

M T W T F
● ● ● ●
Screen Breaks
Afternoon
Fresh Air
● ● ●
M T W

Period/Subject

Teacher Check-in
M T W T F
○ ○ ○ ○ ○

Class Attendance
M T W T F
○ ○ ○ ○ ○ *in person*
○ ○ ○ ○ ○ *online*

Notes & Assignments

— *Important* —

Period/Subject

Teacher Check-in
M T W T F
○ ○ ○ ○ ○

Class Attendance
M T W T F
○ ○ ○ ○ ○ *in person*
○ ○ ○ ○ ○ *online*

Notes & Assignments

— *Important* —

J·F·M·A·M·J·J·A·S·O·N·D

_TO_

_____,

Biggest fish to fry this week

Weekly goals (& whatnot)

1

2

3

4

5

It was the best of times . . .

. . . It was the worst of times

Parent check~in
(How is your plague?)

	The rash is gone!	Slightly flushed	A few pustules	Throw me on the cart
S	○	○	○	○
M	○	○	○	○
T	○	○	○	○
W	○	○	○	○
T	○	○	○	○
F	○	○	○	○
S	○	○	○	○

Student check~in
(How are the humours?)

	Sprightly!	Fair	A bit lethargic	The bile is black
S	○	○	○	○
M	○	○	○	○
T	○	○	○	○
W	○	○	○	○
T	○	○	○	○
F	○	○	○	○
S	○	○	○	○

Tolling of the bell
(School day routine)

Time	Activity	M	T	W	T	F
		☐	☐	☐	☐	☐
		☐	☐	☐	☐	☐
		☐	☐	☐	☐	☐
		☐	☐	☐	☐	☐
		☐	☐	☐	☐	☐
		☐	☐	☐	☐	☐
		☐	☐	☐	☐	☐
		☐	☐	☐	☐	☐
		☐	☐	☐	☐	☐
		☐	☐	☐	☐	☐
		☐	☐	☐	☐	☐
		☐	☐	☐	☐	☐
		☐	☐	☐	☐	☐
		☐	☐	☐	☐	☐
		☐	☐	☐	☐	☐
		☐	☐	☐	☐	☐
		☐	☐	☐	☐	☐

Saturday	Sunday

Bird's~eye view of the week
(A glimpse from the top of the tower)

Monday	Tuesday	Wednesday	Thursday	Friday

Weekly Class Notes

Period/Subject

Teacher Check-in
M T W T F
○ ○ ○ ○ ○

Class Attendance
M T W T F
○ ○ ○ ○ ○ *in person*
○ ○ ○ ○ ○ *online*

Notes & Assignments

— Important —

Period/Subject

Teacher Check-in
M T W T F
○ ○ ○ ○ ○

Class Attendance
M T W T F
○ ○ ○ ○ ○ *in person*
○ ○ ○ ○ ○ *online*

Notes & Assignments

— Important —

Screen Breaks
— *Morning* —
Fresh Air

Period/Subject

Teacher Check-in
M T W T F
○ ○ ○ ○ ○

Class Attendance
M T W T F
○ ○ ○ ○ ○ *in person*
○ ○ ○ ○ ○ *online*

Notes & Assignments

— Important —

Period/Subject

Teacher Check-in
M T W T F
○ ○ ○ ○ ○

Class Attendance
M T W T F
○ ○ ○ ○ ○ *in person*
○ ○ ○ ○ ○ *online*

Notes & Assignments

— Important —

Weekly Class Notes

Period/Subject

Teacher Check-in
M T W T F
○ ○ ○ ○ ○

Class Attendance
M T W T F
○ ○ ○ ○ ○ — *in person*
○ ○ ○ ○ ○ — *online*

Notes & Assignments

- [ ]
- [ ]
- [ ]
- [ ]
- [ ]
- [ ]
- [ ]

— *Important* —

Period/Subject

Teacher Check-in
M T W T F
○ ○ ○ ○ ○

Class Attendance
M T W T F
○ ○ ○ ○ ○ — *in person*
○ ○ ○ ○ ○ — *online*

Notes & Assignments

- [ ]
- [ ]
- [ ]
- [ ]
- [ ]
- [ ]
- [ ]

— *Important* —

M T W T F
● ● ● ● ●
Screen Breaks
Afternoon
Fresh Air
● ● ● ● ●
M T W T F

Period/Subject

Teacher Check-in
M T W T F
○ ○ ○ ○ ○

Class Attendance
M T W T F
○ ○ ○ ○ ○ — *in person*
○ ○ ○ ○ ○ — *online*

Notes & Assignments

- [ ]
- [ ]
- [ ]
- [ ]
- [ ]
- [ ]
- [ ]

— *Important* —

Period/Subject

Teacher Check-in
M T W T F
○ ○ ○ ○ ○

Class Attendance
M T W T F
○ ○ ○ ○ ○ — *in person*
○ ○ ○ ○ ○ — *online*

Notes & Assignments

- [ ]
- [ ]
- [ ]
- [ ]
- [ ]
- [ ]
- [ ]

— *Important* —

J·F·M·A·M·J·J·A·S·O·N·D

_TO_

_____,

Biggest fish to fry this week

It was the best of times . . .

. . . It was the worst of times

Weekly goals (& whatnot)

1

      2

3

      4

5

Parent check~in
(How is your plague?)

	The rash is gone!	Slightly flushed	A few pustules	Throw me on the cart
S	○	○	○	○
M	○	○	○	○
T	○	○	○	○
W	○	○	○	○
T	○	○	○	○
F	○	○	○	○
S	○	○	○	○

Student check~in
(How are the humours?)

	Sprightly!	Fair	A bit lethargic	The bile is black
S	○	○	○	○
M	○	○	○	○
T	○	○	○	○
W	○	○	○	○
T	○	○	○	○
F	○	○	○	○
S	○	○	○	○

Tolling of the bell
(School day routine)

Time	Activity	M	T	W	T	F

Bird's~eye view of the week
(A glimpse from the top of the tower)

Saturday	Sunday

Monday	Tuesday	Wednesday	Thursday	Friday

Weekly Class Notes

Period/Subject

Teacher Check-in
M T W T F
○ ○ ○ ○ ○

Class Attendance
M T W T F
○ ○ ○ ○ ○ *in person*
○ ○ ○ ○ ○ *online*

Notes & Assignments

☐
☐
☐
☐
☐
☐

— *Important* —

Period/Subject

Teacher Check-in
M T W T F
○ ○ ○ ○ ○

Class Attendance
M T W T F
○ ○ ○ ○ ○ *in person*
○ ○ ○ ○ ○ *online*

Notes & Assignments

☐
☐
☐
☐
☐
☐

— *Important* —

Screen Breaks
— *Morning* —
Fresh Air
M T W T F

Period/Subject

Teacher Check-in
M T W T F
○ ○ ○ ○ ○

Class Attendance
M T W T F
○ ○ ○ ○ ○ *in person*
○ ○ ○ ○ ○ *online*

Notes & Assignments

☐
☐
☐
☐
☐
☐

— *Important* —

Period/Subject

Teacher Check-in
M T W T F
○ ○ ○ ○ ○

Class Attendance
M T W T F
○ ○ ○ ○ ○ *in person*
○ ○ ○ ○ ○ *online*

Notes & Assignments

☐
☐
☐
☐
☐
☐

— *Important* —

Weekly Class Notes

Period/Subject

Teacher Check-in
M T W T F
○ ○ ○ ○ ○

Class Attendance
M T W T F
○ ○ ○ ○ ○ *in person*
○ ○ ○ ○ ○ *online*

Notes & Assignments

— *Important* —

Period/Subject

Teacher Check-in
M T W T F
○ ○ ○ ○ ○

Class Attendance
M T W T F
○ ○ ○ ○ ○ *in person*
○ ○ ○ ○ ○ *online*

Notes & Assignments

— *Important* —

Screen Breaks
Afternoon
Fresh Air
M T W T F
M T W T F

Period/Subject

Teacher Check-in
M T W T F
○ ○ ○ ○ ○

Class Attendance
M T W T F
○ ○ ○ ○ ○ *in person*
○ ○ ○ ○ ○ *online*

Notes & Assignments

— *Important* —

Period/Subject

Teacher Check-in
M T W T F
○ ○ ○ ○ ○

Class Attendance
M T W T F
○ ○ ○ ○ ○ *in person*
○ ○ ○ ○ ○ *online*

Notes & Assignments

— *Important* —

J·F·M·A·M·J·J·A·S·O·N·D

_to_

_____ ,

Biggest fish to fry this week

Weekly goals (& whatnot)

1

     2

3

     4

5

It was the best of times . . .

. . . It was the worst of times

Parent check~in
(How is your plague?)

	The rash is gone!	Slightly flushed	A few pustules	Throw me on the cart
S	○	○	○	○
M	○	○	○	○
T	○	○	○	○
W	○	○	○	○
T	○	○	○	○
F	○	○	○	○
S	○	○	○	○

Student check~in
(How are the humours?)

	Sprightly!	Fair	A bit lethargic	The bile is black
S	○	○	○	○
M	○	○	○	○
T	○	○	○	○
W	○	○	○	○
T	○	○	○	○
F	○	○	○	○
S	○	○	○	○

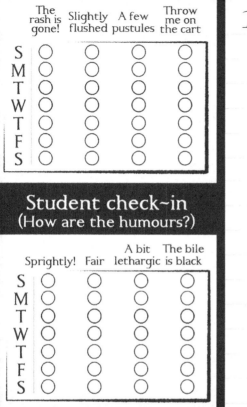

Tolling of the bell
(School day routine)

Time	Activity	M	T	W	T	F

Saturday	Sunday

Bird's~eye view of the week
(A glimpse from the top of the tower)

Monday	Tuesday	Wednesday	Thursday	Friday

Weekly Class Notes

Period/Subject

Teacher Check-in
M T W T F
○ ○ ○ ○ ○

Class Attendance
M T W T F
○ ○ ○ ○ ○ in person
○ ○ ○ ○ ○ online

Notes & Assignments

☐
☐
☐
☐
☐
☐
☐

— Important —

Period/Subject

Teacher Check-in
M T W T F
○ ○ ○ ○ ○

Class Attendance
M T W T F
○ ○ ○ ○ ○ in person
○ ○ ○ ○ ○ online

Notes & Assignments

☐
☐
☐
☐
☐
☐
☐

— Important —

Screen Breaks
— *Morning* —
Fresh Air

M W T F
○ ○ ○ ○

M T W
○ ○ ○

Period/Subject

Teacher Check-in
M T W T F
○ ○ ○ ○ ○

Class Attendance
M T W T F
○ ○ ○ ○ ○ in person
○ ○ ○ ○ ○ online

Notes & Assignments

☐
☐
☐
☐
☐
☐
☐

— Important —

Period/Subject

Teacher Check-in
M T W T F
○ ○ ○ ○ ○

Class Attendance
M T W T F
○ ○ ○ ○ ○ in person
○ ○ ○ ○ ○ online

Notes & Assignments

☐
☐
☐
☐
☐
☐
☐

— Important —

Weekly Class Notes

Period/Subject

Teacher Check-in

M T W T F
○ ○ ○ ○ ○

Class Attendance

M T W T F
○ ○ ○ ○ ○ *in person*
○ ○ ○ ○ ○ *online*

Notes & Assignments

— *Important* —

Period/Subject

Teacher Check-in

M T W T F
○ ○ ○ ○ ○

Class Attendance

M T W T F
○ ○ ○ ○ ○ *in person*
○ ○ ○ ○ ○ *online*

Notes & Assignments

— *Important* —

Screen Breaks
Afternoon
Fresh Air

M T W T F

M T W T F

Period/Subject

Teacher Check-in

M T W T F
○ ○ ○ ○ ○

Class Attendance

M T W T F
○ ○ ○ ○ ○ *in person*
○ ○ ○ ○ ○ *online*

Notes & Assignments

— *Important* —

Period/Subject

Teacher Check-in

M T W T F
○ ○ ○ ○ ○

Class Attendance

M T W T F
○ ○ ○ ○ ○ *in person*
○ ○ ○ ○ ○ *online*

Notes & Assignments

— *Important* —

J·F·M·A·M·J·J·A·S·O·N·D

_TO_

_____ ,

Biggest fish to
fry this week

It was the best of times . . .

. . . It was the worst of times

Weekly goals (& whatnot)

1

      2

3

      4

5

Parent check~in
(How is your plague?)

	The rash is gone!	Slightly flushed	A few pustules	Throw me on the cart
S	○	○	○	○
M	○	○	○	○
T	○	○	○	○
W	○	○	○	○
T	○	○	○	○
F	○	○	○	○
S	○	○	○	○

Student check~in
(How are the humours?)

	Sprightly!	Fair	A bit lethargic	The bile is black
S	○	○	○	○
M	○	○	○	○
T	○	○	○	○
W	○	○	○	○
T	○	○	○	○
F	○	○	○	○
S	○	○	○	○

Tolling of the bell
(School day routine)

Time	Activity	M	T	W	T	F

	Saturday	Sunday

Bird's~eye view of the week
(A glimpse from the top of the tower)

Monday	Tuesday	Wednesday	Thursday	Friday

Weekly Class Notes

Period/Subject

Teacher Check-in
M T W T F
○ ○ ○ ○ ○

Class Attendance
M T W T F
○ ○ ○ ○ ○ *in person*
○ ○ ○ ○ ○ *online*

Notes & Assignments

☐
☐
☐
☐
☐
☐

— Important —

Period/Subject

Teacher Check-in
M T W T F
○ ○ ○ ○ ○

Class Attendance
M T W T F
○ ○ ○ ○ ○ *in person*
○ ○ ○ ○ ○ *online*

Notes & Assignments

☐
☐
☐
☐
☐
☐

— Important —

M T W T F
● ● ●
● ●
Screen Breaks
— Morning —
Fresh Air
● ●
● ●
M T W T F
W

Period/Subject

Teacher Check-in
M T W T F
○ ○ ○ ○ ○

Class Attendance
M T W T F
○ ○ ○ ○ ○ *in person*
○ ○ ○ ○ ○ *online*

Notes & Assignments

☐
☐
☐
☐
☐
☐

— Important —

Period/Subject

Teacher Check-in
M T W T F
○ ○ ○ ○ ○

Class Attendance
M T W T F
○ ○ ○ ○ ○ *in person*
○ ○ ○ ○ ○ *online*

Notes & Assignments

☐
☐
☐
☐
☐
☐

— Important —

Weekly Class Notes

Period/Subject

Teacher Check-in
M T W T F
○ ○ ○ ○ ○

Class Attendance
M T W T F
○ ○ ○ ○ ○   in person
○ ○ ○ ○ ○   online

Notes & Assignments

— Important —

Period/Subject

Teacher Check-in
M T W T F
○ ○ ○ ○ ○

Class Attendance
M T W T F
○ ○ ○ ○ ○   in person
○ ○ ○ ○ ○   online

Notes & Assignments

— Important —

Screen Breaks
Afternoon
Fresh Air

M T W T F

Period/Subject

Teacher Check-in
M T W T F
○ ○ ○ ○ ○

Class Attendance
M T W T F
○ ○ ○ ○ ○   in person
○ ○ ○ ○ ○   online

Notes & Assignments

— Important —

Period/Subject

Teacher Check-in
M T W T F
○ ○ ○ ○ ○

Class Attendance
M T W T F
○ ○ ○ ○ ○   in person
○ ○ ○ ○ ○   online

Notes & Assignments

— Important —

J·F·M·A·M·J·J·A·S·O·N·D

_____ TO _____ ,

Biggest fish to fry this week

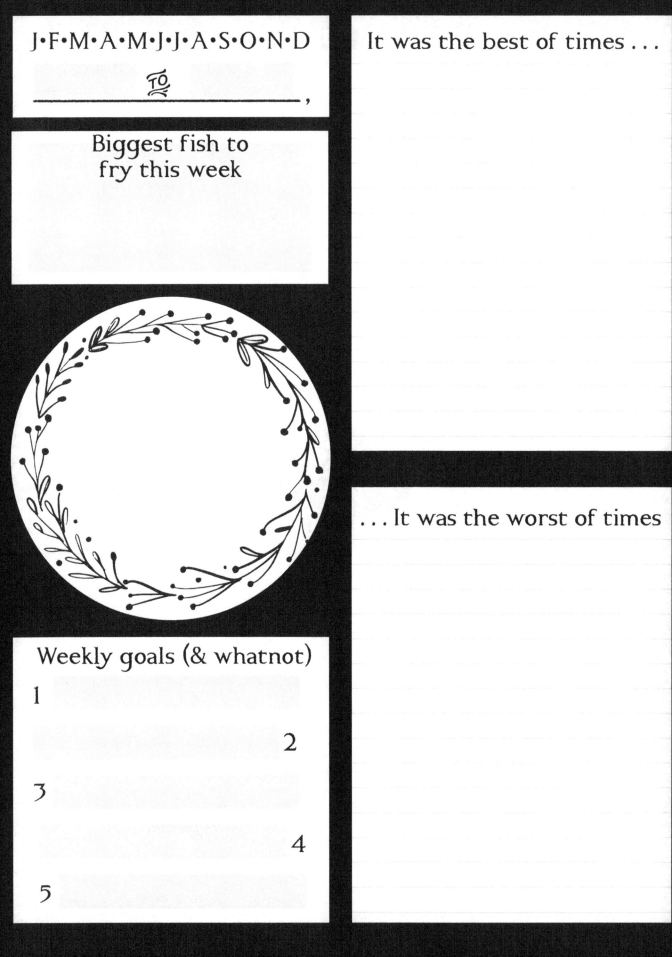

It was the best of times . . .

. . . It was the worst of times

Weekly goals (& whatnot)

1

2

3

4

5

Parent check~in
(How is your plague?)

	The rash is gone!	Slightly flushed	A few pustules	Throw me on the cart
S	○	○	○	○
M	○	○	○	○
T	○	○	○	○
W	○	○	○	○
T	○	○	○	○
F	○	○	○	○
S	○	○	○	○

Student check~in
(How are the humours?)

	Sprightly!	Fair	A bit lethargic	The bile is black
S	○	○	○	○
M	○	○	○	○
T	○	○	○	○
W	○	○	○	○
T	○	○	○	○
F	○	○	○	○
S	○	○	○	○

Tolling of the bell
(School day routine)

Time	*Activity*	M	T	W	T	F
		☐	☐	☐	☐	☐
		☐	☐	☐	☐	☐
		☐	☐	☐	☐	☐
		☐	☐	☐	☐	☐
		☐	☐	☐	☐	☐
		☐	☐	☐	☐	☐
		☐	☐	☐	☐	☐
		☐	☐	☐	☐	☐
		☐	☐	☐	☐	☐
		☐	☐	☐	☐	☐
		☐	☐	☐	☐	☐
		☐	☐	☐	☐	☐
		☐	☐	☐	☐	☐
		☐	☐	☐	☐	☐
		☐	☐	☐	☐	☐
		☐	☐	☐	☐	☐
		☐	☐	☐	☐	☐
		☐	☐	☐	☐	☐

Saturday	Sunday

Bird's~eye view of the week
(A glimpse from the top of the tower)

Monday	Tuesday	Wednesday	Thursday	Friday

Weekly Class Notes

Period/Subject

Teacher Check-in
M T W T F
○ ○ ○ ○ ○

Class Attendance
M T W T F
○ ○ ○ ○ ○ *in person*
○ ○ ○ ○ ○ *online*

Notes & Assignments

☐
☐
☐
☐
☐
☐

— *Important* —

Period/Subject

Teacher Check-in
M T W T F
○ ○ ○ ○ ○

Class Attendance
M T W T F
○ ○ ○ ○ ○ *in person*
○ ○ ○ ○ ○ *online*

Notes & Assignments

☐
☐
☐
☐
☐
☐

— *Important* —

Screen Breaks
— *Morning* —
Fresh Air
M T W T F

Period/Subject

Teacher Check-in
M T W T F
○ ○ ○ ○ ○

Class Attendance
M T W T F
○ ○ ○ ○ ○ *in person*
○ ○ ○ ○ ○ *online*

Notes & Assignments

☐
☐
☐
☐
☐
☐

— *Important* —

Period/Subject

Teacher Check-in
M T W T F
○ ○ ○ ○ ○

Class Attendance
M T W T F
○ ○ ○ ○ ○ *in person*
○ ○ ○ ○ ○ *online*

Notes & Assignments

☐
☐
☐
☐
☐
☐

— *Important* —

Weekly Class Notes

Period/Subject

Teacher Check-in
M T W T F
○ ○ ○ ○ ○

Class Attendance
M T W T F
○ ○ ○ ○ ○ in person
○ ○ ○ ○ ○ online

Notes & Assignments

— Important —

Period/Subject

Teacher Check-in
M T W T F
○ ○ ○ ○ ○

Class Attendance
M T W T F
○ ○ ○ ○ ○ in person
○ ○ ○ ○ ○ online

Notes & Assignments

— Important —

Screen Breaks
Afternoon
Fresh Air

Period/Subject

Teacher Check-in
M T W T F
○ ○ ○ ○ ○

Class Attendance
M T W T F
○ ○ ○ ○ ○ in person
○ ○ ○ ○ ○ online

Notes & Assignments

— Important —

Period/Subject

Teacher Check-in
M T W T F
○ ○ ○ ○ ○

Class Attendance
M T W T F
○ ○ ○ ○ ○ in person
○ ○ ○ ○ ○ online

Notes & Assignments

— Important —

J·F·M·A·M·J·J·A·S·O·N·D

 TO

_____ ,

Biggest fish to fry this week

Weekly goals (& whatnot)

1

2

3

4

5

It was the best of times . . .

. . . It was the worst of times

Parent check~in
(How is your plague?)

	The rash is gone!	Slightly flushed	A few pustules	Throw me on the cart
S	○	○	○	○
M	○	○	○	○
T	○	○	○	○
W	○	○	○	○
T	○	○	○	○
F	○	○	○	○
S	○	○	○	○

Student check~in
(How are the humours?)

	Sprightly!	Fair	A bit lethargic	The bile is black
S	○	○	○	○
M	○	○	○	○
T	○	○	○	○
W	○	○	○	○
T	○	○	○	○
F	○	○	○	○
S	○	○	○	○

Tolling of the bell
(School day routine)

Time	Activity	M	T	W	T	F
		☐	☐	☐	☐	☐
		☐	☐	☐	☐	☐
		☐	☐	☐	☐	☐
		☐	☐	☐	☐	☐
		☐	☐	☐	☐	☐
		☐	☐	☐	☐	☐
		☐	☐	☐	☐	☐
		☐	☐	☐	☐	☐
		☐	☐	☐	☐	☐
		☐	☐	☐	☐	☐
		☐	☐	☐	☐	☐
		☐	☐	☐	☐	☐
		☐	☐	☐	☐	☐
		☐	☐	☐	☐	☐
		☐	☐	☐	☐	☐
		☐	☐	☐	☐	☐

Saturday	Sunday

Bird's~eye view of the week
(A glimpse from the top of the tower)

Monday	Tuesday	Wednesday	Thursday	Friday

Weekly Class Notes

Period/Subject

Teacher Check-in
M T W T F
○ ○ ○ ○ ○

Class Attendance
M T W T F
○ ○ ○ ○ ○ *in person*
○ ○ ○ ○ ○ *online*

Notes & Assignments

— *Important* —

Period/Subject

Teacher Check-in
M T W T F
○ ○ ○ ○ ○

Class Attendance
M T W T F
○ ○ ○ ○ ○ *in person*
○ ○ ○ ○ ○ *online*

Notes & Assignments

— *Important* —

Screen Breaks
— *Morning* —
Fresh Air
M T W T F

Period/Subject

Teacher Check-in
M T W T F
○ ○ ○ ○ ○

Class Attendance
M T W T F
○ ○ ○ ○ ○ *in person*
○ ○ ○ ○ ○ *online*

Notes & Assignments

— *Important* —

Period/Subject

Teacher Check-in
M T W T F
○ ○ ○ ○ ○

Class Attendance
M T W T F
○ ○ ○ ○ ○ *in person*
○ ○ ○ ○ ○ *online*

Notes & Assignments

— *Important* —

Weekly Class Notes

Period/Subject

Teacher Check-in
M T W T F
○ ○ ○ ○ ○

Class Attendance
M T W T F
○ ○ ○ ○ ○ *in person*
○ ○ ○ ○ ○ *online*

Notes & Assignments

— *Important* —

Period/Subject

Teacher Check-in
M T W T F
○ ○ ○ ○ ○

Class Attendance
M T W T F
○ ○ ○ ○ ○ *in person*
○ ○ ○ ○ ○ *online*

Notes & Assignments

— *Important* —

Screen Breaks
Afternoon
Fresh Air

M T W T F

Period/Subject

Teacher Check-in
M T W T F
○ ○ ○ ○ ○

Class Attendance
M T W T F
○ ○ ○ ○ ○ *in person*
○ ○ ○ ○ ○ *online*

Notes & Assignments

— *Important* —

Period/Subject

Teacher Check-in
M T W T F
○ ○ ○ ○ ○

Class Attendance
M T W T F
○ ○ ○ ○ ○ *in person*
○ ○ ○ ○ ○ *online*

Notes & Assignments

— *Important* —

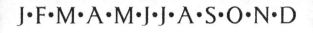

J·F·M·A·M·J·J·A·S·O·N·D

_____ TO _____,

Biggest fish to fry this week

It was the best of times . . .

. . . It was the worst of times

Weekly goals (& whatnot)

1

2

3

4

5

Parent check~in
(How is your plague?)

	The rash is gone!	Slightly flushed	A few pustules	Throw me on the cart
S	○	○	○	○
M	○	○	○	○
T	○	○	○	○
W	○	○	○	○
T	○	○	○	○
F	○	○	○	○
S	○	○	○	○

Student check~in
(How are the humours?)

	Sprightly!	Fair	A bit lethargic	The bile is black
S	○	○	○	○
M	○	○	○	○
T	○	○	○	○
W	○	○	○	○
T	○	○	○	○
F	○	○	○	○
S	○	○	○	○

Tolling of the bell
(School day routine)

Time	Activity	M	T	W	T	F

Saturday	Sunday

Bird's~eye view of the week
(A glimpse from the top of the tower)

Monday	Tuesday	Wednesday	Thursday	Friday

Weekly Class Notes

Period/Subject

Teacher Check-in
M T W T F
○ ○ ○ ○ ○

Class Attendance
M T W T F
○ ○ ○ ○ ○ *in person*
○ ○ ○ ○ ○ *online*

Notes & Assignments

— *Important* —

Period/Subject

Teacher Check-in
M T W T F
○ ○ ○ ○ ○

Class Attendance
M T W T F
○ ○ ○ ○ ○ *in person*
○ ○ ○ ○ ○ *online*

Notes & Assignments

— *Important* —

Screen Breaks
M T W T F

Morning

Fresh Air
M T W T F

Period/Subject

Teacher Check-in
M T W T F
○ ○ ○ ○ ○

Class Attendance
M T W T F
○ ○ ○ ○ ○ *in person*
○ ○ ○ ○ ○ *online*

Notes & Assignments

— *Important* —

Period/Subject

Teacher Check-in
M T W T F
○ ○ ○ ○ ○

Class Attendance
M T W T F
○ ○ ○ ○ ○ *in person*
○ ○ ○ ○ ○ *online*

Notes & Assignments

— *Important* —

Weekly Class Notes

Period/Subject

Teacher Check-in
M T W T F
○ ○ ○ ○ ○

Class Attendance
M T W T F
○ ○ ○ ○ ○ *in person*
○ ○ ○ ○ ○ *online*

Notes & Assignments

— Important —

Period/Subject

Teacher Check-in
M T W T F
○ ○ ○ ○ ○

Class Attendance
M T W T F
○ ○ ○ ○ ○ *in person*
○ ○ ○ ○ ○ *online*

Notes & Assignments

— Important —

M T W T F
Screen Breaks
Afternoon
Fresh Air
M T W T F

Period/Subject

Teacher Check-in
M T W T F
○ ○ ○ ○ ○

Class Attendance
M T W T F
○ ○ ○ ○ ○ *in person*
○ ○ ○ ○ ○ *online*

Notes & Assignments

— Important —

Period/Subject

Teacher Check-in
M T W T F
○ ○ ○ ○ ○

Class Attendance
M T W T F
○ ○ ○ ○ ○ *in person*
○ ○ ○ ○ ○ *online*

Notes & Assignments

— Important —

J·F·M·A·M·J·J·A·S·O·N·D

_TO_

_____ ,

Biggest fish to
fry this week

Weekly goals (& whatnot)

1

2

3

4

5

It was the best of times . . .

. . . It was the worst of times

Parent check~in
(How is your plague?)

	The rash is gone!	Slightly flushed	A few pustules	Throw me on the cart
S	○	○	○	○
M	○	○	○	○
T	○	○	○	○
W	○	○	○	○
T	○	○	○	○
F	○	○	○	○
S	○	○	○	○

Student check~in
(How are the humours?)

	Sprightly!	Fair	A bit lethargic	The bile is black
S	○	○	○	○
M	○	○	○	○
T	○	○	○	○
W	○	○	○	○
T	○	○	○	○
F	○	○	○	○
S	○	○	○	○

Tolling of the bell
(School day routine)

Time	Activity	M	T	W	T	F
		☐	☐	☐	☐	☐
		☐	☐	☐	☐	☐
		☐	☐	☐	☐	☐
		☐	☐	☐	☐	☐
		☐	☐	☐	☐	☐
		☐	☐	☐	☐	☐
		☐	☐	☐	☐	☐
		☐	☐	☐	☐	☐
		☐	☐	☐	☐	☐
		☐	☐	☐	☐	☐
		☐	☐	☐	☐	☐
		☐	☐	☐	☐	☐
		☐	☐	☐	☐	☐
		☐	☐	☐	☐	☐
		☐	☐	☐	☐	☐
		☐	☐	☐	☐	☐
		☐	☐	☐	☐	☐

Saturday	Sunday

Bird's~eye view of the week
(A glimpse from the top of the tower)

Monday	Tuesday	Wednesday	Thursday	Friday

Weekly Class Notes

Period/Subject

Teacher Check-in
M T W T F
○ ○ ○ ○ ○

Class Attendance
M T W T F
○ ○ ○ ○ ○ *in person*
○ ○ ○ ○ ○ *online*

Notes & Assignments

— *Important* —

Period/Subject

Teacher Check-in
M T W T F
○ ○ ○ ○ ○

Class Attendance
M T W T F
○ ○ ○ ○ ○ *in person*
○ ○ ○ ○ ○ *online*

Notes & Assignments

— *Important* —

Screen Breaks
— *Morning* —
Fresh Air

Period/Subject

Teacher Check-in
M T W T F
○ ○ ○ ○ ○

Class Attendance
M T W T F
○ ○ ○ ○ ○ *in person*
○ ○ ○ ○ ○ *online*

Notes & Assignments

— *Important* —

Period/Subject

Teacher Check-in
M T W T F
○ ○ ○ ○ ○

Class Attendance
M T W T F
○ ○ ○ ○ ○ *in person*
○ ○ ○ ○ ○ *online*

Notes & Assignments

— *Important* —

Weekly Class Notes

Period/Subject

Teacher Check-in
M T W T F
○ ○ ○ ○ ○

Class Attendance
M T W T F
○ ○ ○ ○ ○ *in person*
○ ○ ○ ○ ○ *online*

Notes & Assignments

— *Important* —

Period/Subject

Teacher Check-in
M T W T F
○ ○ ○ ○ ○

Class Attendance
M T W T F
○ ○ ○ ○ ○ *in person*
○ ○ ○ ○ ○ *online*

Notes & Assignments

— *Important* —

Screen Breaks
Afternoon
Fresh Air

Period/Subject

Teacher Check-in
M T W T F
○ ○ ○ ○ ○

Class Attendance
M T W T F
○ ○ ○ ○ ○ *in person*
○ ○ ○ ○ ○ *online*

Notes & Assignments

— *Important* —

Period/Subject

Teacher Check-in
M T W T F
○ ○ ○ ○ ○

Class Attendance
M T W T F
○ ○ ○ ○ ○ *in person*
○ ○ ○ ○ ○ *online*

Notes & Assignments

— *Important* —

J·F·M·A·M·J·J·A·S·O·N·D

_TO_

_____ ,

Biggest fish to
fry this week

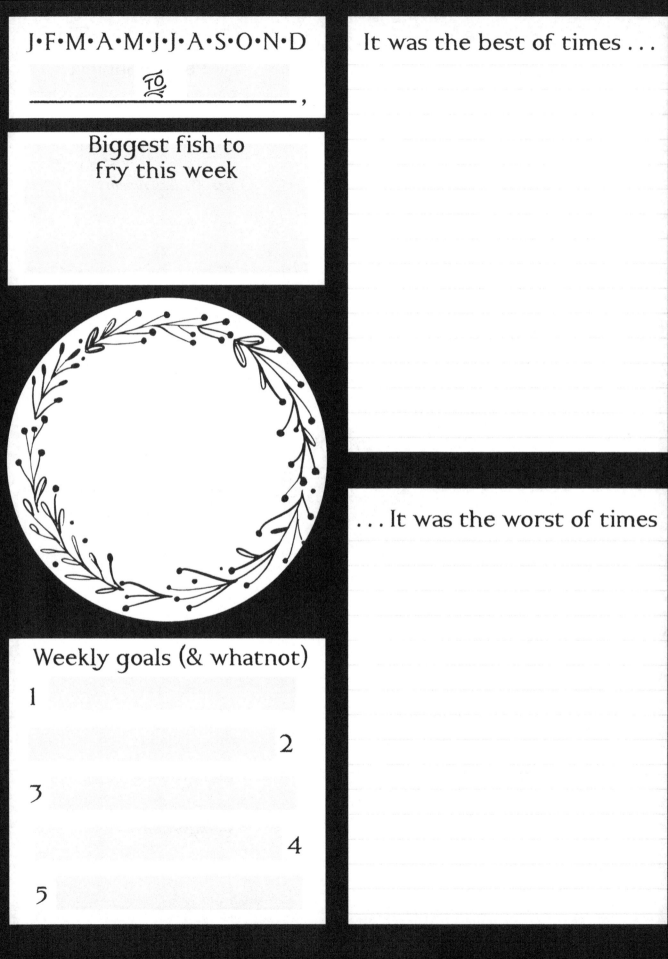

Weekly goals (& whatnot)

1

2

3

4

5

It was the best of times . . .

. . . It was the worst of times

Parent check~in
(How is your plague?)

	The rash is gone!	Slightly flushed	A few pustules	Throw me on the cart
S	○	○	○	○
M	○	○	○	○
T	○	○	○	○
W	○	○	○	○
T	○	○	○	○
F	○	○	○	○
S	○	○	○	○

Student check~in
(How are the humours?)

	Sprightly!	Fair	A bit lethargic	The bile is black
S	○	○	○	○
M	○	○	○	○
T	○	○	○	○
W	○	○	○	○
T	○	○	○	○
F	○	○	○	○
S	○	○	○	○

Tolling of the bell
(School day routine)

Time	Activity	M	T	W	T	F

Saturday	Sunday

Bird's~eye view of the week
(A glimpse from the top of the tower)

Monday	Tuesday	Wednesday	Thursday	Friday

Weekly Class Notes

Period/Subject

Teacher Check-in
M T W T F
○ ○ ○ ○ ○

Class Attendance
M T W T F
○ ○ ○ ○ ○ in person
○ ○ ○ ○ ○ online

Notes & Assignments

— Important —

Period/Subject

Teacher Check-in
M T W T F
○ ○ ○ ○ ○

Class Attendance
M T W T F
○ ○ ○ ○ ○ in person
○ ○ ○ ○ ○ online

Notes & Assignments

— Important —

Screen Breaks
Morning
Fresh Air

Period/Subject

Teacher Check-in
M T W T F
○ ○ ○ ○ ○

Class Attendance
M T W T F
○ ○ ○ ○ ○ in person
○ ○ ○ ○ ○ online

Notes & Assignments

— Important —

Period/Subject

Teacher Check-in
M T W T F
○ ○ ○ ○ ○

Class Attendance
M T W T F
○ ○ ○ ○ ○ in person
○ ○ ○ ○ ○ online

Notes & Assignments

— Important —

Weekly Class Notes

Period/Subject

Teacher Check-in
M T W T F
○ ○ ○ ○ ○

Class Attendance
M T W T F
○ ○ ○ ○ ○ *in person*
○ ○ ○ ○ ○ *online*

Notes & Assignments

— *Important* —

Period/Subject

Teacher Check-in
M T W T F
○ ○ ○ ○ ○

Class Attendance
M T W T F
○ ○ ○ ○ ○ *in person*
○ ○ ○ ○ ○ *online*

Notes & Assignments

— *Important* —

Screen Breaks
Afternoon
Fresh Air
M T W T F
M T W T F

Period/Subject

Teacher Check-in
M T W T F
○ ○ ○ ○ ○

Class Attendance
M T W T F
○ ○ ○ ○ ○ *in person*
○ ○ ○ ○ ○ *online*

Notes & Assignments

— *Important* —

Period/Subject

Teacher Check-in
M T W T F
○ ○ ○ ○ ○

Class Attendance
M T W T F
○ ○ ○ ○ ○ *in person*
○ ○ ○ ○ ○ *online*

Notes & Assignments

— *Important* —

J·F·M·A·M·J·J·A·S·O·N·D

_____ TO _____,

Biggest fish to fry this week

Weekly goals (& whatnot)

1

2

3

4

5

It was the best of times . . .

. . . It was the worst of times

Parent check~in
(How is your plague?)

	The rash is gone!	Slightly flushed	A few pustules	Throw me on the cart
S	○	○	○	○
M	○	○	○	○
T	○	○	○	○
W	○	○	○	○
T	○	○	○	○
F	○	○	○	○
S	○	○	○	○

Student check~in
(How are the humours?)

	Sprightly!	Fair	A bit lethargic	The bile is black
S	○	○	○	○
M	○	○	○	○
T	○	○	○	○
W	○	○	○	○
T	○	○	○	○
F	○	○	○	○
S	○	○	○	○

Tolling of the bell
(School day routine)

Time	Activity	M	T	W	T	F
		☐	☐	☐	☐	☐
		☐	☐	☐	☐	☐
		☐	☐	☐	☐	☐
		☐	☐	☐	☐	☐
		☐	☐	☐	☐	☐
		☐	☐	☐	☐	☐
		☐	☐	☐	☐	☐
		☐	☐	☐	☐	☐
		☐	☐	☐	☐	☐
		☐	☐	☐	☐	☐
		☐	☐	☐	☐	☐
		☐	☐	☐	☐	☐
		☐	☐	☐	☐	☐
		☐	☐	☐	☐	☐
		☐	☐	☐	☐	☐
		☐	☐	☐	☐	☐
		☐	☐	☐	☐	☐
		☐	☐	☐	☐	☐

Saturday	Sunday

Bird's~eye view of the week
(A glimpse from the top of the tower)

Monday	Tuesday	Wednesday	Thursday	Friday

Weekly Class Notes

Period/Subject

Teacher Check-in
M T W T F
○ ○ ○ ○ ○

Class Attendance
M T W T F
○ ○ ○ ○ ○ *in person*
○ ○ ○ ○ ○ *online*

Notes & Assignments

— *Important* —

Period/Subject

Teacher Check-in
M T W T F
○ ○ ○ ○ ○

Class Attendance
M T W T F
○ ○ ○ ○ ○ *in person*
○ ○ ○ ○ ○ *online*

Notes & Assignments

— *Important* —

M T W T F
Screen Breaks
— *Morning* —
Fresh Air
M T W T F

Period/Subject

Teacher Check-in
M T W T F
○ ○ ○ ○ ○

Class Attendance
M T W T F
○ ○ ○ ○ ○ *in person*
○ ○ ○ ○ ○ *online*

Notes & Assignments

— *Important* —

Period/Subject

Teacher Check-in
M T W T F
○ ○ ○ ○ ○

Class Attendance
M T W T F
○ ○ ○ ○ ○ *in person*
○ ○ ○ ○ ○ *online*

Notes & Assignments

— *Important* —

Weekly Class Notes

Period/Subject

Teacher Check-in
M T W T F
○ ○ ○ ○ ○

Class Attendance
M T W T F
○ ○ ○ ○ ○   in person
○ ○ ○ ○ ○   online

Notes & Assignments

— Important —

Period/Subject

Teacher Check-in
M T W T F
○ ○ ○ ○ ○

Class Attendance
M T W T F
○ ○ ○ ○ ○   in person
○ ○ ○ ○ ○   online

Notes & Assignments

— Important —

Screen Breaks
— *Afternoon* —
Fresh Air

Period/Subject

Teacher Check-in
M T W T F
○ ○ ○ ○ ○

Class Attendance
M T W T F
○ ○ ○ ○ ○   in person
○ ○ ○ ○ ○   online

Notes & Assignments

— Important —

Period/Subject

Teacher Check-in
M T W T F
○ ○ ○ ○ ○

Class Attendance
M T W T F
○ ○ ○ ○ ○   in person
○ ○ ○ ○ ○   online

Notes & Assignments

— Important —

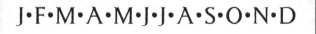

J·F·M·A·M·J·J·A·S·O·N·D

_TO_

_____ ,

Biggest fish to fry this week

Weekly goals (& whatnot)

1

                       2

3

                       4

5

It was the best of times . . .

. . . It was the worst of times

Parent check~in
(How is your plague?)

	The rash is gone!	Slightly flushed	A few pustules	Throw me on the cart
S	○	○	○	○
M	○	○	○	○
T	○	○	○	○
W	○	○	○	○
T	○	○	○	○
F	○	○	○	○
S	○	○	○	○

Student check~in
(How are the humours?)

	Sprightly!	Fair	A bit lethargic	The bile is black
S	○	○	○	○
M	○	○	○	○
T	○	○	○	○
W	○	○	○	○
T	○	○	○	○
F	○	○	○	○
S	○	○	○	○

Tolling of the bell
(School day routine)

Time	Activity	M	T	W	T	F

	Saturday	Sunday

Bird's~eye view of the week
(A glimpse from the top of the tower)

Monday	Tuesday	Wednesday	Thursday	Friday

Weekly Class Notes

Period/Subject

Teacher Check-in
M T W T F
○ ○ ○ ○ ○

Class Attendance
M T W T F
○ ○ ○ ○ ○ in person
○ ○ ○ ○ ○ online

Notes & Assignments

☐
☐
☐
☐
☐
☐
☐

— *Important* —

Period/Subject

Teacher Check-in
M T W T F
○ ○ ○ ○ ○

Class Attendance
M T W T F
○ ○ ○ ○ ○ in person
○ ○ ○ ○ ○ online

Notes & Assignments

☐
☐
☐
☐
☐

— *Important* —

Screen Breaks
— *Morning* —
Fresh Air

Period/Subject

Teacher Check-in
M T W T F
○ ○ ○ ○ ○

Class Attendance
M T W T F
○ ○ ○ ○ ○ in person
○ ○ ○ ○ ○ online

Notes & Assignments

☐
☐
☐
☐
☐
☐
☐

— *Important* —

Period/Subject

Teacher Check-in
M T W T F
○ ○ ○ ○ ○

Class Attendance
M T W T F
○ ○ ○ ○ ○ in person
○ ○ ○ ○ ○ online

Notes & Assignments

☐
☐
☐
☐
☐

— *Important* —

Weekly Class Notes

Period/Subject

Teacher Check-in
M T W T F
○ ○ ○ ○ ○

Class Attendance
M T W T F
○ ○ ○ ○ ○ — *in person*
○ ○ ○ ○ ○ — *online*

Notes & Assignments

— *Important* —

Period/Subject

Teacher Check-in
M T W T F
○ ○ ○ ○ ○

Class Attendance
M T W T F
○ ○ ○ ○ ○ — *in person*
○ ○ ○ ○ ○ — *online*

Notes & Assignments

— *Important* —

Screen Breaks
— *Afternoon* —
Fresh Air

M T W T F

Period/Subject

Teacher Check-in
M T W T F
○ ○ ○ ○ ○

Class Attendance
M T W T F
○ ○ ○ ○ ○ — *in person*
○ ○ ○ ○ ○ — *online*

Notes & Assignments

— *Important* —

Period/Subject

Teacher Check-in
M T W T F
○ ○ ○ ○ ○

Class Attendance
M T W T F
○ ○ ○ ○ ○ — *in person*
○ ○ ○ ○ ○ — *online*

Notes & Assignments

— *Important* —

J·F·M·A·M·J·J·A·S·O·N·D

_TO_

_____ ,

Biggest fish to
fry this week

Weekly goals (& whatnot)

1

2

3

4

5

It was the best of times . . .

. . . It was the worst of times

Parent check~in
(How is your plague?)

	The rash is gone!	Slightly flushed	A few pustules	Throw me on the cart
S	○	○	○	○
M	○	○	○	○
T	○	○	○	○
W	○	○	○	○
T	○	○	○	○
F	○	○	○	○
S	○	○	○	○

Student check~in
(How are the humours?)

	Sprightly!	Fair	A bit lethargic	The bile is black
S	○	○	○	○
M	○	○	○	○
T	○	○	○	○
W	○	○	○	○
T	○	○	○	○
F	○	○	○	○
S	○	○	○	○

Tolling of the bell
(School day routine)

Time	Activity	M	T	W	T	F

Saturday	Sunday

Bird's~eye view of the week
(A glimpse from the top of the tower)

Monday	Tuesday	Wednesday	Thursday	Friday

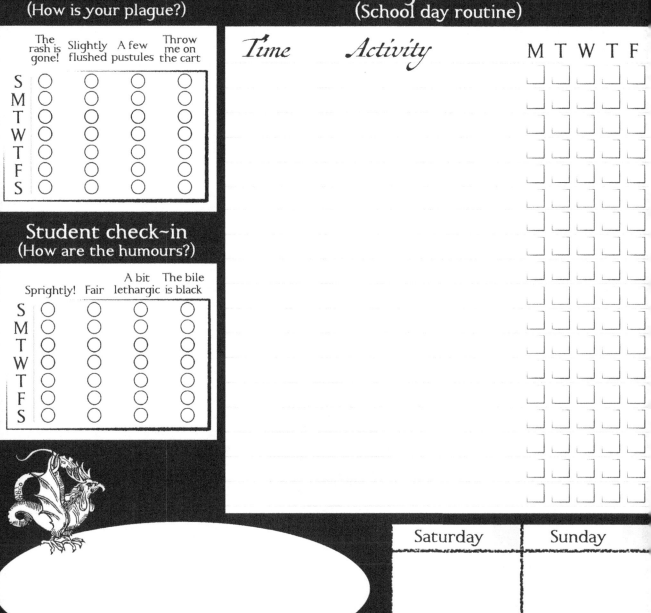

Weekly Class Notes

Period/Subject

Teacher Check-in
M T W T F
○ ○ ○ ○ ○

Class Attendance
M T W T F
○ ○ ○ ○ ○ *in person*
○ ○ ○ ○ ○ *online*

Notes & Assignments

☐
☐
☐
☐
☐
☐
☐

— Important —

Period/Subject

Teacher Check-in
M T W T F
○ ○ ○ ○ ○

Class Attendance
M T W T F
○ ○ ○ ○ ○ *in person*
○ ○ ○ ○ ○ *online*

Notes & Assignments

☐
☐
☐
☐
☐
☐
☐

— Important —

M T W T F
● ● ●
● ●
Screen Breaks
— Morning —
Fresh Air
● ●
M T ● W T F

Period/Subject

Teacher Check-in
M T W T F
○ ○ ○ ○ ○

Class Attendance
M T W T F
○ ○ ○ ○ ○ *in person*
○ ○ ○ ○ ○ *online*

Notes & Assignments

☐
☐
☐
☐
☐
☐

— Important —

Period/Subject

Teacher Check-in
M T W T F
○ ○ ○ ○ ○

Class Attendance
M T W T F
○ ○ ○ ○ ○ *in person*
○ ○ ○ ○ ○ *online*

Notes & Assignments

☐
☐
☐
☐
☐
☐

— Important —

Weekly Class Notes

Period/Subject

Teacher Check-in
M T W T F
○ ○ ○ ○ ○

Class Attendance
M T W T F
○ ○ ○ ○ ○ *in person*
○ ○ ○ ○ ○ *online*

Notes & Assignments

☐
☐
☐
☐
☐
☐
☐

— *Important* —

Period/Subject

Teacher Check-in
M T W T F
○ ○ ○ ○ ○

Class Attendance
M T W T F
○ ○ ○ ○ ○ *in person*
○ ○ ○ ○ ○ *online*

Notes & Assignments

☐
☐
☐
☐
☐

— *Important* —

Screen Breaks
— *Afternoon* —
Fresh Air

Period/Subject

Teacher Check-in
M T W T F
○ ○ ○ ○ ○

Class Attendance
M T W T F
○ ○ ○ ○ ○ *in person*
○ ○ ○ ○ ○ *online*

Notes & Assignments

☐
☐
☐
☐
☐
☐

— *Important* —

Period/Subject

Teacher Check-in
M T W T F
○ ○ ○ ○ ○

Class Attendance
M T W T F
○ ○ ○ ○ ○ *in person*
○ ○ ○ ○ ○ *online*

Notes & Assignments

☐
☐
☐
☐
☐

— *Important* —

J·F·M·A·M·J·J·A·S·O·N·D

TO

_____,

Biggest fish to fry this week

It was the best of times . . .

. . . It was the worst of times

Weekly goals (& whatnot)

1

2

3

4

5

Parent check~in
(How is your plague?)

	The rash is gone!	Slightly flushed	A few pustules	Throw me on the cart
S	○	○	○	○
M	○	○	○	○
T	○	○	○	○
W	○	○	○	○
T	○	○	○	○
F	○	○	○	○
S	○	○	○	○

Student check~in
(How are the humours?)

	Sprightly!	Fair	A bit lethargic	The bile is black
S	○	○	○	○
M	○	○	○	○
T	○	○	○	○
W	○	○	○	○
T	○	○	○	○
F	○	○	○	○
S	○	○	○	○

Tolling of the bell
(School day routine)

Time	Activity	M	T	W	T	F

Saturday	Sunday

Bird's~eye view of the week
(A glimpse from the top of the tower)

Monday	Tuesday	Wednesday	Thursday	Friday

Weekly Class Notes

Period/Subject

Teacher Check-in
M T W T F
○ ○ ○ ○ ○

Class Attendance
M T W T F
○ ○ ○ ○ ○   in person
○ ○ ○ ○ ○   online

Notes & Assignments

☐
☐
☐
☐
☐
☐
☐

— Important —

Period/Subject

Teacher Check-in
M T W T F
○ ○ ○ ○ ○

Class Attendance
M T W T F
○ ○ ○ ○ ○   in person
○ ○ ○ ○ ○   online

Notes & Assignments

☐
☐
☐
☐
☐
☐
☐

— Important —

W T F
M T
Screen Breaks
— *Morning* —
Fresh Air
T F
M W

Period/Subject

Teacher Check-in
M T W T F
○ ○ ○ ○ ○

Class Attendance
M T W T F
○ ○ ○ ○ ○   in person
○ ○ ○ ○ ○   online

Notes & Assignments

☐
☐
☐
☐
☐
☐
☐

— Important —

Period/Subject

Teacher Check-in
M T W T F
○ ○ ○ ○ ○

Class Attendance
M T W T F
○ ○ ○ ○ ○   in person
○ ○ ○ ○ ○   online

Notes & Assignments

☐
☐
☐
☐
☐
☐
☐

— Important —

Weekly Class Notes

Period/Subject

Teacher Check-in
M T W T F
○ ○ ○ ○ ○

Class Attendance
M T W T F
○ ○ ○ ○ ○ in person
○ ○ ○ ○ ○ online

Notes & Assignments

— *Important* —

Period/Subject

Teacher Check-in
M T W T F
○ ○ ○ ○ ○

Class Attendance
M T W T F
○ ○ ○ ○ ○ in person
○ ○ ○ ○ ○ online

Notes & Assignments

— *Important* —

Screen Breaks
Afternoon
Fresh Air

Period/Subject

Teacher Check-in
M T W T F
○ ○ ○ ○ ○

Class Attendance
M T W T F
○ ○ ○ ○ ○ in person
○ ○ ○ ○ ○ online

Notes & Assignments

— *Important* —

Period/Subject

Teacher Check-in
M T W T F
○ ○ ○ ○ ○

Class Attendance
M T W T F
○ ○ ○ ○ ○ in person
○ ○ ○ ○ ○ online

Notes & Assignments

— *Important* —

J·F·M·A·M·J·J·A·S·O·N·D

_TO_

_____ ,

Biggest fish to fry this week

Weekly goals (& whatnot)

1

2

3

4

5

It was the best of times . . .

. . . It was the worst of times

Parent check~in
(How is your plague?)

	The rash is gone!	Slightly flushed	A few pustules	Throw me on the cart
S	○	○	○	○
M	○	○	○	○
T	○	○	○	○
W	○	○	○	○
T	○	○	○	○
F	○	○	○	○
S	○	○	○	○

Student check~in
(How are the humours?)

	Sprightly!	Fair	A bit lethargic	The bile is black
S	○	○	○	○
M	○	○	○	○
T	○	○	○	○
W	○	○	○	○
T	○	○	○	○
F	○	○	○	○
S	○	○	○	○

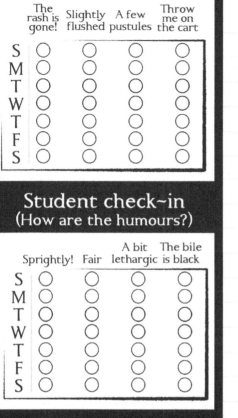

Tolling of the bell
(School day routine)

Time	Activity	M	T	W	T	F
		☐	☐	☐	☐	☐
		☐	☐	☐	☐	☐
		☐	☐	☐	☐	☐
		☐	☐	☐	☐	☐
		☐	☐	☐	☐	☐
		☐	☐	☐	☐	☐
		☐	☐	☐	☐	☐
		☐	☐	☐	☐	☐
		☐	☐	☐	☐	☐
		☐	☐	☐	☐	☐
		☐	☐	☐	☐	☐
		☐	☐	☐	☐	☐
		☐	☐	☐	☐	☐
		☐	☐	☐	☐	☐
		☐	☐	☐	☐	☐
		☐	☐	☐	☐	☐
		☐	☐	☐	☐	☐
		☐	☐	☐	☐	☐

Saturday	Sunday

Bird's~eye view of the week
(A glimpse from the top of the tower)

Monday	Tuesday	Wednesday	Thursday	Friday

Weekly Class Notes

Period/Subject

Teacher Check-in
M T W T F
○ ○ ○ ○ ○

Class Attendance
M T W T F
○ ○ ○ ○ ○ *in person*
○ ○ ○ ○ ○ *online*

Notes & Assignments

— Important —

Period/Subject

Teacher Check-in
M T W T F
○ ○ ○ ○ ○

Class Attendance
M T W T F
○ ○ ○ ○ ○ *in person*
○ ○ ○ ○ ○ *online*

Notes & Assignments

— Important —

Screen Breaks
M T W T F
— Morning —
Fresh Air
M T W T F

Period/Subject

Teacher Check-in
M T W T F
○ ○ ○ ○ ○

Class Attendance
M T W T F
○ ○ ○ ○ ○ *in person*
○ ○ ○ ○ ○ *online*

Notes & Assignments

— Important —

Period/Subject

Teacher Check-in
M T W T F
○ ○ ○ ○ ○

Class Attendance
M T W T F
○ ○ ○ ○ ○ *in person*
○ ○ ○ ○ ○ *online*

Notes & Assignments

— Important —

Weekly Class Notes

Period/Subject

Teacher Check-in
M T W T F
○ ○ ○ ○ ○

Class Attendance
M T W T F
○ ○ ○ ○ ○   *in person*
○ ○ ○ ○ ○   *online*

Notes & Assignments

— *Important* —

Period/Subject

Teacher Check-in
M T W T F
○ ○ ○ ○ ○

Class Attendance
M T W T F
○ ○ ○ ○ ○   *in person*
○ ○ ○ ○ ○   *online*

Notes & Assignments

— *Important* —

M T W T F
Screen Breaks
Afternoon
Fresh Air
M T W T F

Period/Subject

Teacher Check-in
M T W T F
○ ○ ○ ○ ○

Class Attendance
M T W T F
○ ○ ○ ○ ○   *in person*
○ ○ ○ ○ ○   *online*

Notes & Assignments

— *Important* —

Period/Subject

Teacher Check-in
M T W T F
○ ○ ○ ○ ○

Class Attendance
M T W T F
○ ○ ○ ○ ○   *in person*
○ ○ ○ ○ ○   *online*

Notes & Assignments

— *Important* —

J·F·M·A·M·J·J·A·S·O·N·D

_TO_

_____ ,

Biggest fish to fry this week

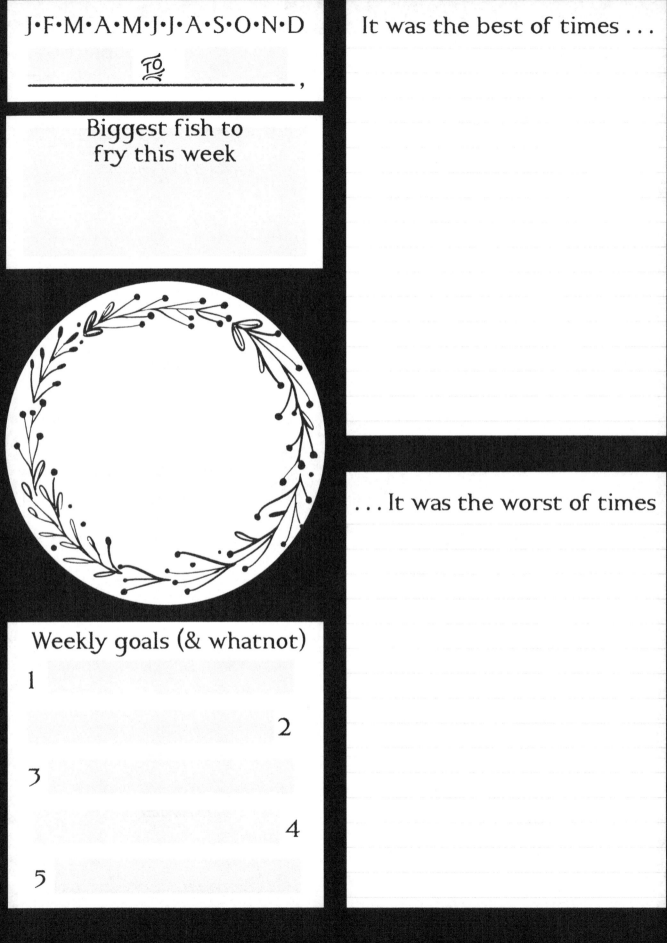

Weekly goals (& whatnot)

1

2

3

4

5

It was the best of times . . .

. . . It was the worst of times

Parent check~in
(How is your plague?)

	The rash is gone!	Slightly flushed	A few pustules	Throw me on the cart
S	○	○	○	○
M	○	○	○	○
T	○	○	○	○
W	○	○	○	○
T	○	○	○	○
F	○	○	○	○
S	○	○	○	○

Student check~in
(How are the humours?)

	Sprightly!	Fair	A bit lethargic	The bile is black
S	○	○	○	○
M	○	○	○	○
T	○	○	○	○
W	○	○	○	○
T	○	○	○	○
F	○	○	○	○
S	○	○	○	○

Tolling of the bell
(School day routine)

Time	Activity	M	T	W	T	F

Saturday	Sunday

Bird's~eye view of the week
(A glimpse from the top of the tower)

Monday	Tuesday	Wednesday	Thursday	Friday

Weekly Class Notes

Period/Subject

Teacher Check-in
M T W T F
○ ○ ○ ○ ○

Class Attendance
M T W T F
○ ○ ○ ○ ○ *in person*
○ ○ ○ ○ ○ *online*

Notes & Assignments

— Important —

Period/Subject

Teacher Check-in
M T W T F
○ ○ ○ ○ ○

Class Attendance
M T W T F
○ ○ ○ ○ ○ *in person*
○ ○ ○ ○ ○ *online*

Notes & Assignments

— Important —

Screen Breaks
Morning
Fresh Air
M T W T F

Period/Subject

Teacher Check-in
M T W T F
○ ○ ○ ○ ○

Class Attendance
M T W T F
○ ○ ○ ○ ○ *in person*
○ ○ ○ ○ ○ *online*

Notes & Assignments

— Important —

Period/Subject

Teacher Check-in
M T W T F
○ ○ ○ ○ ○

Class Attendance
M T W T F
○ ○ ○ ○ ○ *in person*
○ ○ ○ ○ ○ *online*

Notes & Assignments

— Important —

Weekly Class Notes

Period/Subject

Teacher Check-in
M T W T F
○ ○ ○ ○ ○

Class Attendance
M T W T F
○ ○ ○ ○ ○ *in person*
○ ○ ○ ○ ○ *online*

Notes & Assignments

— *Important* —

Period/Subject

Teacher Check-in
M T W T F
○ ○ ○ ○ ○

Class Attendance
M T W T F
○ ○ ○ ○ ○ *in person*
○ ○ ○ ○ ○ *online*

Notes & Assignments

— *Important* —

Screen Breaks
M T W T F
— Afternoon —
Fresh Air
M T W T F

Period/Subject

Teacher Check-in
M T W T F
○ ○ ○ ○ ○

Class Attendance
M T W T F
○ ○ ○ ○ ○ *in person*
○ ○ ○ ○ ○ *online*

Notes & Assignments

— *Important* —

Period/Subject

Teacher Check-in
M T W T F
○ ○ ○ ○ ○

Class Attendance
M T W T F
○ ○ ○ ○ ○ *in person*
○ ○ ○ ○ ○ *online*

Notes & Assignments

— *Important* —

J·F·M·A·M·J·J·A·S·O·N·D

_____ TO _____ ,

Biggest fish to fry this week

Weekly goals (& whatnot)

1

2

3

4

5

It was the best of times . . .

. . . It was the worst of times

Parent check~in
(How is your plague?)

	The rash is gone!	Slightly flushed	A few pustules	Throw me on the cart
S	○	○	○	○
M	○	○	○	○
T	○	○	○	○
W	○	○	○	○
T	○	○	○	○
F	○	○	○	○
S	○	○	○	○

Student check~in
(How are the humours?)

	Sprightly!	Fair	A bit lethargic	The bile is black
S	○	○	○	○
M	○	○	○	○
T	○	○	○	○
W	○	○	○	○
T	○	○	○	○
F	○	○	○	○
S	○	○	○	○

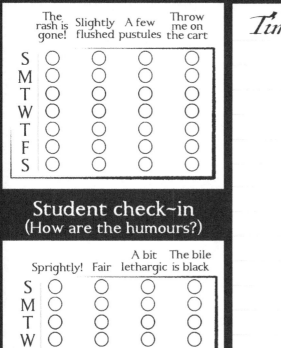

Tolling of the bell
(School day routine)

Time	*Activity*	M	T	W	T	F

Saturday	Sunday

Bird's~eye view of the week
(A glimpse from the top of the tower)

Monday	Tuesday	Wednesday	Thursday	Friday

Weekly Class Notes

Period/Subject

Teacher Check-in
M T W T F
○ ○ ○ ○ ○

Class Attendance
M T W T F
○ ○ ○ ○ ○ *in person*
○ ○ ○ ○ ○ *online*

Notes & Assignments

— *Important* —

Period/Subject

Teacher Check-in
M T W T F
○ ○ ○ ○ ○

Class Attendance
M T W T F
○ ○ ○ ○ ○ *in person*
○ ○ ○ ○ ○ *online*

Notes & Assignments

— *Important* —

Screen Breaks
Morning
Fresh Air

Period/Subject

Teacher Check-in
M T W T F
○ ○ ○ ○ ○

Class Attendance
M T W T F
○ ○ ○ ○ ○ *in person*
○ ○ ○ ○ ○ *online*

Notes & Assignments

— *Important* —

Period/Subject

Teacher Check-in
M T W T F
○ ○ ○ ○ ○

Class Attendance
M T W T F
○ ○ ○ ○ ○ *in person*
○ ○ ○ ○ ○ *online*

Notes & Assignments

— *Important* —

Weekly Class Notes

Period/Subject

Teacher Check-in
M T W T F
○ ○ ○ ○ ○

Class Attendance
M T W T F
○ ○ ○ ○ ○   in person
○ ○ ○ ○ ○   online

Notes & Assignments

— Important —

Period/Subject

Teacher Check-in
M T W T F
○ ○ ○ ○ ○

Class Attendance
M T W T F
○ ○ ○ ○ ○   in person
○ ○ ○ ○ ○   online

Notes & Assignments

— Important —

Screen Breaks
— *Afternoon* —
Fresh Air

Period/Subject

Teacher Check-in
M T W T F
○ ○ ○ ○ ○

Class Attendance
M T W T F
○ ○ ○ ○ ○   in person
○ ○ ○ ○ ○   online

Notes & Assignments

— Important —

Period/Subject

Teacher Check-in
M T W T F
○ ○ ○ ○ ○

Class Attendance
M T W T F
○ ○ ○ ○ ○   in person
○ ○ ○ ○ ○   online

Notes & Assignments

— Important —

J·F·M·A·M·J·J·A·S·O·N·D

_____ TO _____ ,

Biggest fish to
fry this week

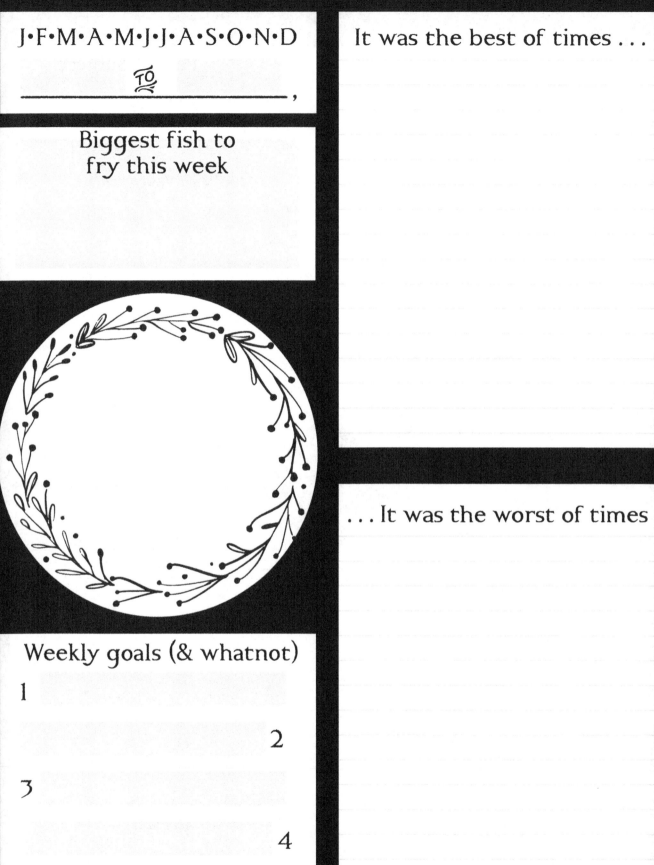

Weekly goals (& whatnot)

1

2

3

4

5

It was the best of times . . .

. . . It was the worst of times

Parent check~in
(How is your plague?)

	The rash is gone!	Slightly flushed	A few pustules	Throw me on the cart
S	○	○	○	○
M	○	○	○	○
T	○	○	○	○
W	○	○	○	○
T	○	○	○	○
F	○	○	○	○
S	○	○	○	○

Student check~in
(How are the humours?)

	Sprightly!	Fair	A bit lethargic	The bile is black
S	○	○	○	○
M	○	○	○	○
T	○	○	○	○
W	○	○	○	○
T	○	○	○	○
F	○	○	○	○
S	○	○	○	○

Tolling of the bell
(School day routine)

Time	Activity	M	T	W	T	F
		☐	☐	☐	☐	☐
		☐	☐	☐	☐	☐
		☐	☐	☐	☐	☐
		☐	☐	☐	☐	☐
		☐	☐	☐	☐	☐
		☐	☐	☐	☐	☐
		☐	☐	☐	☐	☐
		☐	☐	☐	☐	☐
		☐	☐	☐	☐	☐
		☐	☐	☐	☐	☐
		☐	☐	☐	☐	☐
		☐	☐	☐	☐	☐
		☐	☐	☐	☐	☐
		☐	☐	☐	☐	☐
		☐	☐	☐	☐	☐
		☐	☐	☐	☐	☐
		☐	☐	☐	☐	☐

Saturday	Sunday

Bird's~eye view of the week
(A glimpse from the top of the tower)

Monday	Tuesday	Wednesday	Thursday	Friday

Weekly Class Notes

Period/Subject

Teacher Check-in
M T W T F
○ ○ ○ ○ ○

Class Attendance
M T W T F
○ ○ ○ ○ ○ *in person*
○ ○ ○ ○ ○ *online*

Notes & Assignments

- [ ]
- [ ]
- [ ]
- [ ]
- [ ]
- [ ]
- [ ]

— *Important* —

Period/Subject

Teacher Check-in
M T W T F
○ ○ ○ ○ ○

Class Attendance
M T W T F
○ ○ ○ ○ ○ *in person*
○ ○ ○ ○ ○ *online*

Notes & Assignments

- [ ]
- [ ]
- [ ]
- [ ]
- [ ]
- [ ]
- [ ]

— *Important* —

Screen Breaks
Morning
Fresh Air

Period/Subject

Teacher Check-in
M T W T F
○ ○ ○ ○ ○

Class Attendance
M T W T F
○ ○ ○ ○ ○ *in person*
○ ○ ○ ○ ○ *online*

Notes & Assignments

- [ ]
- [ ]
- [ ]
- [ ]
- [ ]
- [ ]
- [ ]

— *Important* —

Period/Subject

Teacher Check-in
M T W T F
○ ○ ○ ○ ○

Class Attendance
M T W T F
○ ○ ○ ○ ○ *in person*
○ ○ ○ ○ ○ *online*

Notes & Assignments

- [ ]
- [ ]
- [ ]
- [ ]
- [ ]
- [ ]
- [ ]

— *Important* —

Weekly Class Notes

Period/Subject

Teacher Check-in
M T W T F
○ ○ ○ ○ ○

Class Attendance
M T W T F
○ ○ ○ ○ ○ *in person*
○ ○ ○ ○ ○ *online*

Notes & Assignments

☐
☐
☐
☐
☐
☐
☐

— Important —

Period/Subject

Teacher Check-in
M T W T F
○ ○ ○ ○ ○

Class Attendance
M T W T F
○ ○ ○ ○ ○ *in person*
○ ○ ○ ○ ○ *online*

Notes & Assignments

☐
☐
☐
☐
☐
☐
☐

— Important —

Screen Breaks
— Afternoon —
Fresh Air

M T W T F
M T W T F

Period/Subject

Teacher Check-in
M T W T F
○ ○ ○ ○ ○

Class Attendance
M T W T F
○ ○ ○ ○ ○ *in person*
○ ○ ○ ○ ○ *online*

Notes & Assignments

☐
☐
☐
☐
☐
☐
☐

— Important —

Period/Subject

Teacher Check-in
M T W T F
○ ○ ○ ○ ○

Class Attendance
M T W T F
○ ○ ○ ○ ○ *in person*
○ ○ ○ ○ ○ *online*

Notes & Assignments

☐
☐
☐
☐
☐
☐
☐

— Important —

J·F·M·A·M·J·J·A·S·O·N·D

_TO_

_____ ,

**Biggest fish to
fry this week**

It was the best of times . . .

. . . It was the worst of times

Weekly goals (& whatnot)

1

          2

3

          4

5

Parent check~in
(How is your plague?)

	The rash is gone!	Slightly flushed	A few pustules	Throw me on the cart
S	○	○	○	○
M	○	○	○	○
T	○	○	○	○
W	○	○	○	○
T	○	○	○	○
F	○	○	○	○
S	○	○	○	○

Student check~in
(How are the humours?)

	Sprightly!	Fair	A bit lethargic	The bile is black
S	○	○	○	○
M	○	○	○	○
T	○	○	○	○
W	○	○	○	○
T	○	○	○	○
F	○	○	○	○
S	○	○	○	○

Tolling of the bell
(School day routine)

Time	Activity	M	T	W	T	F

Saturday	Sunday

Bird's~eye view of the week
(A glimpse from the top of the tower)

Monday	Tuesday	Wednesday	Thursday	Friday

Weekly Class Notes

Period/Subject

Teacher Check-in
M T W T F
○ ○ ○ ○ ○

Class Attendance
M T W T F
○ ○ ○ ○ ○ *in person*
○ ○ ○ ○ ○ *online*

Notes & Assignments

☐
☐
☐
☐
☐
☐
☐

— *Important* —

Period/Subject

Teacher Check-in
M T W T F
○ ○ ○ ○ ○

Class Attendance
M T W T F
○ ○ ○ ○ ○ *in person*
○ ○ ○ ○ ○ *online*

Notes & Assignments

☐
☐
☐
☐
☐
☐

— *Important* —

Screen Breaks
M T W T F
— *Morning* —
Fresh Air
M T W T F

Period/Subject

Teacher Check-in
M T W T F
○ ○ ○ ○ ○

Class Attendance
M T W T F
○ ○ ○ ○ ○ *in person*
○ ○ ○ ○ ○ *online*

Notes & Assignments

☐
☐
☐
☐
☐
☐
☐

— *Important* —

Period/Subject

Teacher Check-in
M T W T F
○ ○ ○ ○ ○

Class Attendance
M T W T F
○ ○ ○ ○ ○ *in person*
○ ○ ○ ○ ○ *online*

Notes & Assignments

☐
☐
☐
☐
☐
☐

— *Important* —

Weekly Class Notes

Period/Subject

Teacher Check-in
M T W T F
○ ○ ○ ○ ○

Class Attendance
M T W T F
○ ○ ○ ○ ○ in person
○ ○ ○ ○ ○ online

Notes & Assignments

— Important —

Period/Subject

Teacher Check-in
M T W T F
○ ○ ○ ○ ○

Class Attendance
M T W T F
○ ○ ○ ○ ○ in person
○ ○ ○ ○ ○ online

Notes & Assignments

— Important —

Screen Breaks
M T W T F

— Afternoon —

Fresh Air
M T W T F

Period/Subject

Teacher Check-in
M T W T F
○ ○ ○ ○ ○

Class Attendance
M T W T F
○ ○ ○ ○ ○ in person
○ ○ ○ ○ ○ online

Notes & Assignments

— Important —

Period/Subject

Teacher Check-in
M T W T F
○ ○ ○ ○ ○

Class Attendance
M T W T F
○ ○ ○ ○ ○ in person
○ ○ ○ ○ ○ online

Notes & Assignments

— Important —

J·F·M·A·M·J·J·A·S·O·N·D

_TO_

_____ ,

Biggest fish to fry this week

It was the best of times . . .

Weekly goals (& whatnot)

1

　　　　　　　　　2

3

　　　　　　　　　4

5

. . . It was the worst of times

Parent check~in
(How is your plague?)

	The rash is gone!	Slightly flushed	A few pustules	Throw me on the cart
S	○	○	○	○
M	○	○	○	○
T	○	○	○	○
W	○	○	○	○
T	○	○	○	○
F	○	○	○	○
S	○	○	○	○

Student check~in
(How are the humours?)

	Sprightly!	Fair	A bit lethargic	The bile is black
S	○	○	○	○
M	○	○	○	○
T	○	○	○	○
W	○	○	○	○
T	○	○	○	○
F	○	○	○	○
S	○	○	○	○

Tolling of the bell
(School day routine)

Time	Activity	M	T	W	T	F
		☐	☐	☐	☐	☐
		☐	☐	☐	☐	☐
		☐	☐	☐	☐	☐
		☐	☐	☐	☐	☐
		☐	☐	☐	☐	☐
		☐	☐	☐	☐	☐
		☐	☐	☐	☐	☐
		☐	☐	☐	☐	☐
		☐	☐	☐	☐	☐
		☐	☐	☐	☐	☐
		☐	☐	☐	☐	☐
		☐	☐	☐	☐	☐
		☐	☐	☐	☐	☐
		☐	☐	☐	☐	☐
		☐	☐	☐	☐	☐
		☐	☐	☐	☐	☐
		☐	☐	☐	☐	☐

Saturday	Sunday

Bird's~eye view of the week
(A glimpse from the top of the tower)

Monday	Tuesday	Wednesday	Thursday	Friday

Weekly Class Notes

Period/Subject

Teacher Check-in
M T W T F
○ ○ ○ ○ ○

Class Attendance
M T W T F
○ ○ ○ ○ ○   in person
○ ○ ○ ○ ○   online

Notes & Assignments

☐
☐
☐
☐
☐
☐
☐

— Important —

Period/Subject

Teacher Check-in
M T W T F
○ ○ ○ ○ ○

Class Attendance
M T W T F
○ ○ ○ ○ ○   in person
○ ○ ○ ○ ○   online

Notes & Assignments

☐
☐
☐
☐
☐
☐
☐

— Important —

Screen Breaks
W
M T T F
○ ○ ○ ○ ○
Morning
Fresh Air
○ ○ ○ ○ ○
M T W T F

Period/Subject

Teacher Check-in
M T W T F
○ ○ ○ ○ ○

Class Attendance
M T W T F
○ ○ ○ ○ ○   in person
○ ○ ○ ○ ○   online

Notes & Assignments

☐
☐
☐
☐
☐
☐
☐

— Important —

Period/Subject

Teacher Check-in
M T W T F
○ ○ ○ ○ ○

Class Attendance
M T W T F
○ ○ ○ ○ ○   in person
○ ○ ○ ○ ○   online

Notes & Assignments

☐
☐
☐
☐
☐
☐
☐

— Important —

Weekly Class Notes

Period/Subject

Teacher Check-in
M T W T F
○ ○ ○ ○ ○

Class Attendance
M T W T F
○ ○ ○ ○ ○ *in person*
○ ○ ○ ○ ○ *online*

Notes & Assignments

— *Important* —

Period/Subject

Teacher Check-in
M T W T F
○ ○ ○ ○ ○

Class Attendance
M T W T F
○ ○ ○ ○ ○ *in person*
○ ○ ○ ○ ○ *online*

Notes & Assignments

— *Important* —

Screen Breaks
Afternoon
Fresh Air
M T W T F

Period/Subject

Teacher Check-in
M T W T F
○ ○ ○ ○ ○

Class Attendance
M T W T F
○ ○ ○ ○ ○ *in person*
○ ○ ○ ○ ○ *online*

Notes & Assignments

— *Important* —

Period/Subject

Teacher Check-in
M T W T F
○ ○ ○ ○ ○

Class Attendance
M T W T F
○ ○ ○ ○ ○ *in person*
○ ○ ○ ○ ○ *online*

Notes & Assignments

— *Important* —

J·F·M·A·M·J·J·A·S·O·N·D

_____ TO _____ ,

Biggest fish to fry this week

It was the best of times . . .

. . . It was the worst of times

Weekly goals (& whatnot)

1

2

3

4

5

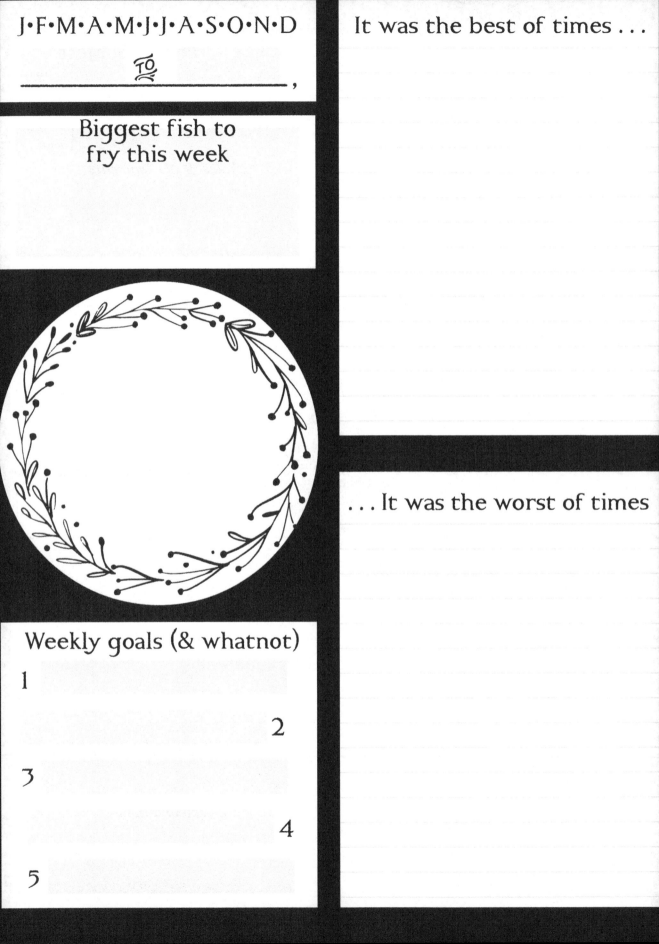

Parent check~in
(How is your plague?)

	The rash is gone!	Slightly flushed	A few pustules	Throw me on the cart
S	○	○	○	○
M	○	○	○	○
T	○	○	○	○
W	○	○	○	○
T	○	○	○	○
F	○	○	○	○
S	○	○	○	○

Student check~in
(How are the humours?)

	Sprightly!	Fair	A bit lethargic	The bile is black
S	○	○	○	○
M	○	○	○	○
T	○	○	○	○
W	○	○	○	○
T	○	○	○	○
F	○	○	○	○
S	○	○	○	○

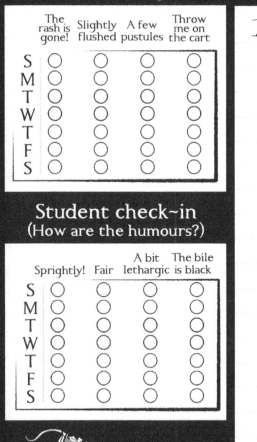

Tolling of the bell
(School day routine)

Time	*Activity*	M	T	W	T	F
		☐	☐	☐	☐	☐
		☐	☐	☐	☐	☐
		☐	☐	☐	☐	☐
		☐	☐	☐	☐	☐
		☐	☐	☐	☐	☐
		☐	☐	☐	☐	☐
		☐	☐	☐	☐	☐
		☐	☐	☐	☐	☐
		☐	☐	☐	☐	☐
		☐	☐	☐	☐	☐
		☐	☐	☐	☐	☐
		☐	☐	☐	☐	☐
		☐	☐	☐	☐	☐
		☐	☐	☐	☐	☐
		☐	☐	☐	☐	☐
		☐	☐	☐	☐	☐
		☐	☐	☐	☐	☐
		☐	☐	☐	☐	☐

Saturday	Sunday

Bird's~eye view of the week
(A glimpse from the top of the tower)

Monday	Tuesday	Wednesday	Thursday	Friday

Weekly Class Notes

Period/Subject

Teacher Check-in
M T W T F
○ ○ ○ ○ ○

Class Attendance
M T W T F
○ ○ ○ ○ ○   *in person*
○ ○ ○ ○ ○   *online*

Notes & Assignments

☐
☐
☐
☐
☐
☐

— Important —

Period/Subject

Teacher Check-in
M T W T F
○ ○ ○ ○ ○

Class Attendance
M T W T F
○ ○ ○ ○ ○   *in person*
○ ○ ○ ○ ○   *online*

Notes & Assignments

☐
☐
☐
☐
☐
☐

— Important —

Screen Breaks
— Morning —
Fresh Air

Period/Subject

Teacher Check-in
M T W T F
○ ○ ○ ○ ○

Class Attendance
M T W T F
○ ○ ○ ○ ○   *in person*
○ ○ ○ ○ ○   *online*

Notes & Assignments

☐
☐
☐
☐
☐
☐

— Important —

Period/Subject

Teacher Check-in
M T W T F
○ ○ ○ ○ ○

Class Attendance
M T W T F
○ ○ ○ ○ ○   *in person*
○ ○ ○ ○ ○   *online*

Notes & Assignments

☐
☐
☐
☐
☐
☐

— Important —

Weekly Class Notes

Period/Subject

Teacher Check-in
M T W T F
○ ○ ○ ○ ○

Class Attendance
M T W T F
○ ○ ○ ○ ○ in person
○ ○ ○ ○ ○ online

Notes & Assignments

— *Important* —

Period/Subject

Teacher Check-in
M T W T F
○ ○ ○ ○ ○

Class Attendance
M T W T F
○ ○ ○ ○ ○ in person
○ ○ ○ ○ ○ online

Notes & Assignments

— *Important* —

Screen Breaks
— *Afternoon* —
Fresh Air

Period/Subject

Teacher Check-in
M T W T F
○ ○ ○ ○ ○

Class Attendance
M T W T F
○ ○ ○ ○ ○ in person
○ ○ ○ ○ ○ online

Notes & Assignments

— *Important* —

Period/Subject

Teacher Check-in
M T W T F
○ ○ ○ ○ ○

Class Attendance
M T W T F
○ ○ ○ ○ ○ in person
○ ○ ○ ○ ○ online

Notes & Assignments

— *Important* —

J·F·M·A·M·J·J·A·S·O·N·D

_____ TO _____ ,

Biggest fish to fry this week

It was the best of times . . .

. . . It was the worst of times

Weekly goals (& whatnot)

1

2

3

4

5

Parent check~in
(How is your plague?)

	The rash is gone!	Slightly flushed	A few pustules	Throw me on the cart
S	○	○	○	○
M	○	○	○	○
T	○	○	○	○
W	○	○	○	○
T	○	○	○	○
F	○	○	○	○
S	○	○	○	○

Student check~in
(How are the humours?)

	Sprightly!	Fair	A bit lethargic	The bile is black
S	○	○	○	○
M	○	○	○	○
T	○	○	○	○
W	○	○	○	○
T	○	○	○	○
F	○	○	○	○
S	○	○	○	○

Tolling of the bell
(School day routine)

Time	Activity	M	T	W	T	F
		☐	☐	☐	☐	☐
		☐	☐	☐	☐	☐
		☐	☐	☐	☐	☐
		☐	☐	☐	☐	☐
		☐	☐	☐	☐	☐
		☐	☐	☐	☐	☐
		☐	☐	☐	☐	☐
		☐	☐	☐	☐	☐
		☐	☐	☐	☐	☐
		☐	☐	☐	☐	☐
		☐	☐	☐	☐	☐
		☐	☐	☐	☐	☐
		☐	☐	☐	☐	☐
		☐	☐	☐	☐	☐
		☐	☐	☐	☐	☐
		☐	☐	☐	☐	☐
		☐	☐	☐	☐	☐
		☐	☐	☐	☐	☐

Saturday	Sunday

Bird's~eye view of the week
(A glimpse from the top of the tower)

Monday	Tuesday	Wednesday	Thursday	Friday

Weekly Class Notes

Period/Subject

Teacher Check-in
M T W T F
○ ○ ○ ○ ○

Class Attendance
M T W T F
○ ○ ○ ○ ○ in person
○ ○ ○ ○ ○ online

Notes & Assignments

☐
☐
☐
☐
☐
☐
☐

— Important —

Period/Subject

Teacher Check-in
M T W T F
○ ○ ○ ○ ○

Class Attendance
M T W T F
○ ○ ○ ○ ○ in person
○ ○ ○ ○ ○ online

Notes & Assignments

☐
☐
☐
☐
☐
☐
☐

— Important —

Screen Breaks
M T W T F
Morning
Fresh Air
M T W T F

Period/Subject

Teacher Check-in
M T W T F
○ ○ ○ ○ ○

Class Attendance
M T W T F
○ ○ ○ ○ ○ in person
○ ○ ○ ○ ○ online

Notes & Assignments

☐
☐
☐
☐
☐
☐
☐

— Important —

Period/Subject

Teacher Check-in
M T W T F
○ ○ ○ ○ ○

Class Attendance
M T W T F
○ ○ ○ ○ ○ in person
○ ○ ○ ○ ○ online

Notes & Assignments

☐
☐
☐
☐
☐
☐
☐

— Important —

Weekly Class Notes

Period/Subject

Teacher Check-in
M T W T F
○ ○ ○ ○ ○

Class Attendance
M T W T F
○ ○ ○ ○ ○ *in person*
○ ○ ○ ○ ○ *online*

Notes & Assignments

☐
☐
☐
☐
☐
☐
☐

— Important —

Period/Subject

Teacher Check-in
M T W T F
○ ○ ○ ○ ○

Class Attendance
M T W T F
○ ○ ○ ○ ○ *in person*
○ ○ ○ ○ ○ *online*

Notes & Assignments

☐
☐
☐
☐
☐
☐
☐

— Important —

Screen Breaks
— Afternoon —
Fresh Air
M T W T F
M T W

Period/Subject

Teacher Check-in
M T W T F
○ ○ ○ ○ ○

Class Attendance
M T W T F
○ ○ ○ ○ ○ *in person*
○ ○ ○ ○ ○ *online*

Notes & Assignments

☐
☐
☐
☐
☐
☐
☐

— Important —

Period/Subject

Teacher Check-in
M T W T F
○ ○ ○ ○ ○

Class Attendance
M T W T F
○ ○ ○ ○ ○ *in person*
○ ○ ○ ○ ○ *online*

Notes & Assignments

☐
☐
☐
☐
☐
☐
☐

— Important —

J·F·M·A·M·J·J·A·S·O·N·D

TO

_____ ,

Biggest fish to
fry this week

It was the best of times . . .

. . . It was the worst of times

Weekly goals (& whatnot)

1

2

3

4

5

Parent check~in
(How is your plague?)

	The rash is gone!	Slightly flushed	A few pustules	Throw me on the cart
S	○	○	○	○
M	○	○	○	○
T	○	○	○	○
W	○	○	○	○
T	○	○	○	○
F	○	○	○	○
S	○	○	○	○

Student check~in
(How are the humours?)

	Sprightly!	Fair	A bit lethargic	The bile is black
S	○	○	○	○
M	○	○	○	○
T	○	○	○	○
W	○	○	○	○
T	○	○	○	○
F	○	○	○	○
S	○	○	○	○

Tolling of the bell
(School day routine)

Time	Activity	M	T	W	T	F

Saturday	Sunday

Bird's~eye view of the week
(A glimpse from the top of the tower)

Monday	Tuesday	Wednesday	Thursday	Friday

Weekly Class Notes

Period/Subject

Teacher Check-in
M T W T F
○ ○ ○ ○ ○

Class Attendance
M T W T F
○ ○ ○ ○ ○ *in person*
○ ○ ○ ○ ○ *online*

Notes & Assignments

— *Important* —

Period/Subject

Teacher Check-in
M T W T F
○ ○ ○ ○ ○

Class Attendance
M T W T F
○ ○ ○ ○ ○ *in person*
○ ○ ○ ○ ○ *online*

Notes & Assignments

— *Important* —

Screen Breaks
Morning
Fresh Air
M T W T F

Period/Subject

Teacher Check-in
M T W T F
○ ○ ○ ○ ○

Class Attendance
M T W T F
○ ○ ○ ○ ○ *in person*
○ ○ ○ ○ ○ *online*

Notes & Assignments

— *Important* —

Period/Subject

Teacher Check-in
M T W T F
○ ○ ○ ○ ○

Class Attendance
M T W T F
○ ○ ○ ○ ○ *in person*
○ ○ ○ ○ ○ *online*

Notes & Assignments

— *Important* —

Weekly Class Notes

Period/Subject

Teacher Check-in
M T W T F
○ ○ ○ ○ ○

Class Attendance
M T W T F
○ ○ ○ ○ ○ in person
○ ○ ○ ○ ○ online

Notes & Assignments

— Important —

Period/Subject

Teacher Check-in
M T W T F
○ ○ ○ ○ ○

Class Attendance
M T W T F
○ ○ ○ ○ ○ in person
○ ○ ○ ○ ○ online

Notes & Assignments

— Important —

Screen Breaks
Afternoon
Fresh Air
M T W T F

Period/Subject

Teacher Check-in
M T W T F
○ ○ ○ ○ ○

Class Attendance
M T W T F
○ ○ ○ ○ ○ in person
○ ○ ○ ○ ○ online

Notes & Assignments

— Important —

Period/Subject

Teacher Check-in
M T W T F
○ ○ ○ ○ ○

Class Attendance
M T W T F
○ ○ ○ ○ ○ in person
○ ○ ○ ○ ○ online

Notes & Assignments

— Important —

J·F·M·A·M·J·J·A·S·O·N·D

TO

_____ ,

Biggest fish to fry this week

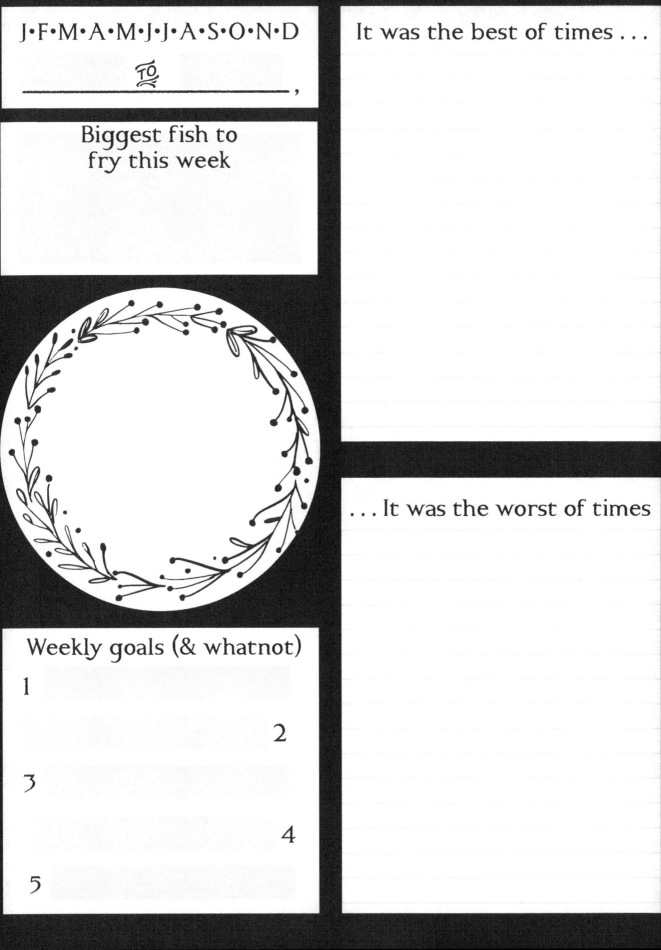

Weekly goals (& whatnot)

1

2

3

4

5

It was the best of times . . .

. . . It was the worst of times

Parent check~in
(How is your plague?)

	The rash is gone!	Slightly flushed	A few pustules	Throw me on the cart
S	○	○	○	○
M	○	○	○	○
T	○	○	○	○
W	○	○	○	○
T	○	○	○	○
F	○	○	○	○
S	○	○	○	○

Student check~in
(How are the humours?)

	Sprightly!	Fair	A bit lethargic	The bile is black
S	○	○	○	○
M	○	○	○	○
T	○	○	○	○
W	○	○	○	○
T	○	○	○	○
F	○	○	○	○
S	○	○	○	○

Tolling of the bell
(School day routine)

Time	Activity	M	T	W	T	F

Saturday	Sunday

Bird's~eye view of the week
(A glimpse from the top of the tower)

Monday	Tuesday	Wednesday	Thursday	Friday

Weekly Class Notes

Period/Subject

Teacher Check-in
M T W T F
○ ○ ○ ○ ○

Class Attendance
M T W T F
○ ○ ○ ○ ○ *in person*
○ ○ ○ ○ ○ *online*

Notes & Assignments

☐
☐
☐
☐
☐
☐
☐

— *Important* —

Period/Subject

Teacher Check-in
M T W T F
○ ○ ○ ○ ○

Class Attendance
M T W T F
○ ○ ○ ○ ○ *in person*
○ ○ ○ ○ ○ *online*

Notes & Assignments

☐
☐
☐
☐
☐
☐
☐

— *Important* —

Screen Breaks
— *Morning* —
Fresh Air
M T W T F

Period/Subject

Teacher Check-in
M T W T F
○ ○ ○ ○ ○

Class Attendance
M T W T F
○ ○ ○ ○ ○ *in person*
○ ○ ○ ○ ○ *online*

Notes & Assignments

☐
☐
☐
☐
☐
☐
☐

— *Important* —

Period/Subject

Teacher Check-in
M T W T F
○ ○ ○ ○ ○

Class Attendance
M T W T F
○ ○ ○ ○ ○ *in person*
○ ○ ○ ○ ○ *online*

Notes & Assignments

☐
☐
☐
☐
☐
☐
☐

— *Important* —

Weekly Class Notes

Period/Subject

Teacher Check-in
M T W T F
○ ○ ○ ○ ○

Class Attendance
M T W T F
○ ○ ○ ○ ○ — in person
○ ○ ○ ○ ○ — online

Notes & Assignments

— Important —

Period/Subject

Teacher Check-in
M T W T F
○ ○ ○ ○ ○

Class Attendance
M T W T F
○ ○ ○ ○ ○ — in person
○ ○ ○ ○ ○ — online

Notes & Assignments

— Important —

Screen Breaks
M T W T F
● ● ● ● ●

Afternoon

Fresh Air
M T W T F
● ● ● ● ●

Period/Subject

Teacher Check-in
M T W T F
○ ○ ○ ○ ○

Class Attendance
M T W T F
○ ○ ○ ○ ○ — in person
○ ○ ○ ○ ○ — online

Notes & Assignments

— Important —

Period/Subject

Teacher Check-in
M T W T F
○ ○ ○ ○ ○

Class Attendance
M T W T F
○ ○ ○ ○ ○ — in person
○ ○ ○ ○ ○ — online

Notes & Assignments

— Important —

J·F·M·A·M·J·J·A·S·O·N·D

TO

_____,

Biggest fish to
fry this week

It was the best of times . . .

. . . It was the worst of times

Weekly goals (& whatnot)

1

2

3

4

5

Parent check~in
(How is your plague?)

	The rash is gone!	Slightly flushed	A few pustules	Throw me on the cart
S	○	○	○	○
M	○	○	○	○
T	○	○	○	○
W	○	○	○	○
T	○	○	○	○
F	○	○	○	○
S	○	○	○	○

Student check~in
(How are the humours?)

	Sprightly!	Fair	A bit lethargic	The bile is black
S	○	○	○	○
M	○	○	○	○
T	○	○	○	○
W	○	○	○	○
T	○	○	○	○
F	○	○	○	○
S	○	○	○	○

Tolling of the bell
(School day routine)

Time	Activity	M	T	W	T	F

Saturday	Sunday

Bird's~eye view of the week
(A glimpse from the top of the tower)

Monday	Tuesday	Wednesday	Thursday	Friday

Weekly Class Notes

Period/Subject

Teacher Check-in
M T W T F
○ ○ ○ ○ ○

Class Attendance
M T W T F
○ ○ ○ ○ ○ *in person*
○ ○ ○ ○ ○ *online*

Notes & Assignments

☐
☐
☐
☐
☐
☐
☐

— *Important* —

Period/Subject

Teacher Check-in
M T W T F
○ ○ ○ ○ ○

Class Attendance
M T W T F
○ ○ ○ ○ ○ *in person*
○ ○ ○ ○ ○ *online*

Notes & Assignments

☐
☐
☐
☐
☐
☐
☐

— *Important* —

Screen Breaks
Morning
Fresh Air

Period/Subject

Teacher Check-in
M T W T F
○ ○ ○ ○ ○

Class Attendance
M T W T F
○ ○ ○ ○ ○ *in person*
○ ○ ○ ○ ○ *online*

Notes & Assignments

☐
☐
☐
☐
☐
☐

— *Important* —

Period/Subject

Teacher Check-in
M T W T F
○ ○ ○ ○ ○

Class Attendance
M T W T F
○ ○ ○ ○ ○ *in person*
○ ○ ○ ○ ○ *online*

Notes & Assignments

☐
☐
☐
☐
☐
☐

— *Important* —

Weekly Class Notes

Period/Subject

Teacher Check-in
M T W T F
○ ○ ○ ○ ○

Class Attendance
M T W T F
○ ○ ○ ○ ○ *in person*
○ ○ ○ ○ ○ *online*

Notes & Assignments

— *Important* —

Period/Subject

Teacher Check-in
M T W T F
○ ○ ○ ○ ○

Class Attendance
M T W T F
○ ○ ○ ○ ○ *in person*
○ ○ ○ ○ ○ *online*

Notes & Assignments

— *Important* —

Screen Breaks
Afternoon
Fresh Air
M T W T F

Period/Subject

Teacher Check-in
M T W T F
○ ○ ○ ○ ○

Class Attendance
M T W T F
○ ○ ○ ○ ○ *in person*
○ ○ ○ ○ ○ *online*

Notes & Assignments

— *Important* —

Period/Subject

Teacher Check-in
M T W T F
○ ○ ○ ○ ○

Class Attendance
M T W T F
○ ○ ○ ○ ○ *in person*
○ ○ ○ ○ ○ *online*

Notes & Assignments

— *Important* —

J·F·M·A·M·J·J·A·S·O·N·D

 _____ ,

Biggest fish to
fry this week

Weekly goals (& whatnot)

1

                              2

3

                              4

5

It was the best of times . . .

. . . It was the worst of times

Parent check~in
(How is your plague?)

	The rash is gone!	Slightly flushed	A few pustules	Throw me on the cart
S	○	○	○	○
M	○	○	○	○
T	○	○	○	○
W	○	○	○	○
T	○	○	○	○
F	○	○	○	○
S	○	○	○	○

Student check~in
(How are the humours?)

	Sprightly!	Fair	A bit lethargic	The bile is black
S	○	○	○	○
M	○	○	○	○
T	○	○	○	○
W	○	○	○	○
T	○	○	○	○
F	○	○	○	○
S	○	○	○	○

Tolling of the bell
(School day routine)

Time	Activity	M	T	W	T	F

Saturday	Sunday

Bird's~eye view of the week
(A glimpse from the top of the tower)

Monday	Tuesday	Wednesday	Thursday	Friday

Weekly Class Notes

Period/Subject

Teacher Check-in
M T W T F
○ ○ ○ ○ ○

Class Attendance
M T W T F
○ ○ ○ ○ ○ *in person*
○ ○ ○ ○ ○ *online*

Notes & Assignments

— *Important* —

Period/Subject

Teacher Check-in
M T W T F
○ ○ ○ ○ ○

Class Attendance
M T W T F
○ ○ ○ ○ ○ *in person*
○ ○ ○ ○ ○ *online*

Notes & Assignments

— *Important* —

Screen Breaks
— *Morning* —
Fresh Air
M T W T F
M T W

Period/Subject

Teacher Check-in
M T W T F
○ ○ ○ ○ ○

Class Attendance
M T W T F
○ ○ ○ ○ ○ *in person*
○ ○ ○ ○ ○ *online*

Notes & Assignments

— *Important* —

Period/Subject

Teacher Check-in
M T W T F
○ ○ ○ ○ ○

Class Attendance
M T W T F
○ ○ ○ ○ ○ *in person*
○ ○ ○ ○ ○ *online*

Notes & Assignments

— *Important* —

Weekly Class Notes

Period/Subject

Teacher Check-in
M T W T F
○ ○ ○ ○ ○

Class Attendance
M T W T F
○ ○ ○ ○ ○   in person
○ ○ ○ ○ ○   online

Notes & Assignments

— Important —

Period/Subject

Teacher Check-in
M T W T F
○ ○ ○ ○ ○

Class Attendance
M T W T F
○ ○ ○ ○ ○   in person
○ ○ ○ ○ ○   online

Notes & Assignments

— Important —

Screen Breaks
— *Afternoon* —
Fresh Air

Period/Subject

Teacher Check-in
M T W T F
○ ○ ○ ○ ○

Class Attendance
M T W T F
○ ○ ○ ○ ○   in person
○ ○ ○ ○ ○   online

Notes & Assignments

— Important —

Period/Subject

Teacher Check-in
M T W T F
○ ○ ○ ○ ○

Class Attendance
M T W T F
○ ○ ○ ○ ○   in person
○ ○ ○ ○ ○   online

Notes & Assignments

— Important —

J·F·M·A·M·J·J·A·S·O·N·D

 TO

_____ ,

Biggest fish to fry this week

Weekly goals (& whatnot)

1

2

3

4

5

It was the best of times . . .

. . . It was the worst of times

Parent check~in
(How is your plague?)

	The rash is gone!	Slightly flushed	A few pustules	Throw me on the cart
S	○	○	○	○
M	○	○	○	○
T	○	○	○	○
W	○	○	○	○
T	○	○	○	○
F	○	○	○	○
S	○	○	○	○

Student check~in
(How are the humours?)

	Sprightly!	Fair	A bit lethargic	The bile is black
S	○	○	○	○
M	○	○	○	○
T	○	○	○	○
W	○	○	○	○
T	○	○	○	○
F	○	○	○	○
S	○	○	○	○

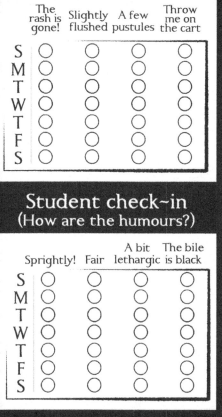

Tolling of the bell
(School day routine)

Time	Activity	M	T	W	T	F

Saturday	Sunday

Bird's~eye view of the week
(A glimpse from the top of the tower)

Monday	Tuesday	Wednesday	Thursday	Friday

Weekly Class Notes

Period/Subject

Teacher Check-in
M T W T F
○ ○ ○ ○ ○

Class Attendance
M T W T F
○ ○ ○ ○ ○ *in person*
○ ○ ○ ○ ○ *online*

Notes & Assignments

□
□
□
□
□
□
□

— *Important* —

Period/Subject

Teacher Check-in
M T W T F
○ ○ ○ ○ ○

Class Attendance
M T W T F
○ ○ ○ ○ ○ *in person*
○ ○ ○ ○ ○ *online*

Notes & Assignments

□
□
□
□
□
□
□

— *Important* —

Screen Breaks
— *Morning* —
Fresh Air

Period/Subject

Teacher Check-in
M T W T F
○ ○ ○ ○ ○

Class Attendance
M T W T F
○ ○ ○ ○ ○ *in person*
○ ○ ○ ○ ○ *online*

Notes & Assignments

□
□
□
□
□
□
□

— *Important* —

Period/Subject

Teacher Check-in
M T W T F
○ ○ ○ ○ ○

Class Attendance
M T W T F
○ ○ ○ ○ ○ *in person*
○ ○ ○ ○ ○ *online*

Notes & Assignments

□
□
□
□
□
□
□

— *Important* —

Weekly Class Notes

Period/Subject

Teacher Check-in
M T W T F
○ ○ ○ ○ ○

Class Attendance
M T W T F
○ ○ ○ ○ ○ in person
○ ○ ○ ○ ○ online

Notes & Assignments

— Important —

Period/Subject

Teacher Check-in
M T W T F
○ ○ ○ ○ ○

Class Attendance
M T W T F
○ ○ ○ ○ ○ in person
○ ○ ○ ○ ○ online

Notes & Assignments

— Important —

Screen Breaks
— *Afternoon* —
Fresh Air

Period/Subject

Teacher Check-in
M T W T F
○ ○ ○ ○ ○

Class Attendance
M T W T F
○ ○ ○ ○ ○ in person
○ ○ ○ ○ ○ online

Notes & Assignments

— Important —

Period/Subject

Teacher Check-in
M T W T F
○ ○ ○ ○ ○

Class Attendance
M T W T F
○ ○ ○ ○ ○ in person
○ ○ ○ ○ ○ online

Notes & Assignments

— Important —

J·F·M·A·M·J·J·A·S·O·N·D

TO

_____ ,

Biggest fish to fry this week

It was the best of times . . .

. . . It was the worst of times

Weekly goals (& whatnot)

1

2

3

4

5

Parent check~in
(How is your plague?)

	The rash is gone!	Slightly flushed	A few pustules	Throw me on the cart
S	○	○	○	○
M	○	○	○	○
T	○	○	○	○
W	○	○	○	○
T	○	○	○	○
F	○	○	○	○
S	○	○	○	○

Student check~in
(How are the humours?)

	Sprightly!	Fair	A bit lethargic	The bile is black
S	○	○	○	○
M	○	○	○	○
T	○	○	○	○
W	○	○	○	○
T	○	○	○	○
F	○	○	○	○
S	○	○	○	○

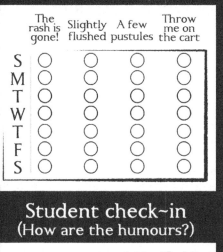

Tolling of the bell
(School day routine)

Time	Activity	M	T	W	T	F
		☐	☐	☐	☐	☐
		☐	☐	☐	☐	☐
		☐	☐	☐	☐	☐
		☐	☐	☐	☐	☐
		☐	☐	☐	☐	☐
		☐	☐	☐	☐	☐
		☐	☐	☐	☐	☐
		☐	☐	☐	☐	☐
		☐	☐	☐	☐	☐
		☐	☐	☐	☐	☐
		☐	☐	☐	☐	☐
		☐	☐	☐	☐	☐
		☐	☐	☐	☐	☐
		☐	☐	☐	☐	☐
		☐	☐	☐	☐	☐
		☐	☐	☐	☐	☐
		☐	☐	☐	☐	☐

Saturday	Sunday

Bird's~eye view of the week
(A glimpse from the top of the tower)

Monday	Tuesday	Wednesday	Thursday	Friday

Weekly Class Notes

Period/Subject

Teacher Check-in
M T W T F
○ ○ ○ ○ ○

Class Attendance
M T W T F
○ ○ ○ ○ ○   in person
○ ○ ○ ○ ○   online

Notes & Assignments

— Important —

Period/Subject

Teacher Check-in
M T W T F
○ ○ ○ ○ ○

Class Attendance
M T W T F
○ ○ ○ ○ ○   in person
○ ○ ○ ○ ○   online

Notes & Assignments

— Important —

Screen Breaks
Morning
Fresh Air

Period/Subject

Teacher Check-in
M T W T F
○ ○ ○ ○ ○

Class Attendance
M T W T F
○ ○ ○ ○ ○   in person
○ ○ ○ ○ ○   online

Notes & Assignments

— Important —

Period/Subject

Teacher Check-in
M T W T F
○ ○ ○ ○ ○

Class Attendance
M T W T F
○ ○ ○ ○ ○   in person
○ ○ ○ ○ ○   online

Notes & Assignments

— Important —

Weekly Class Notes

Period/Subject

Teacher Check-in
M T W T F
○ ○ ○ ○ ○

Class Attendance
M T W T F
○ ○ ○ ○ ○ *in person*
○ ○ ○ ○ ○ *online*

Notes & Assignments

— Important —

Period/Subject

Teacher Check-in
M T W T F
○ ○ ○ ○ ○

Class Attendance
M T W T F
○ ○ ○ ○ ○ *in person*
○ ○ ○ ○ ○ *online*

Notes & Assignments

— Important —

Screen Breaks
Afternoon
Fresh Air
M T W T F

Period/Subject

Teacher Check-in
M T W T F
○ ○ ○ ○ ○

Class Attendance
M T W T F
○ ○ ○ ○ ○ *in person*
○ ○ ○ ○ ○ *online*

Notes & Assignments

— Important —

Period/Subject

Teacher Check-in
M T W T F
○ ○ ○ ○ ○

Class Attendance
M T W T F
○ ○ ○ ○ ○ *in person*
○ ○ ○ ○ ○ *online*

Notes & Assignments

— Important —

J·F·M·A·M·J·J·A·S·O·N·D

_TO_

_____,

Biggest fish to fry this week

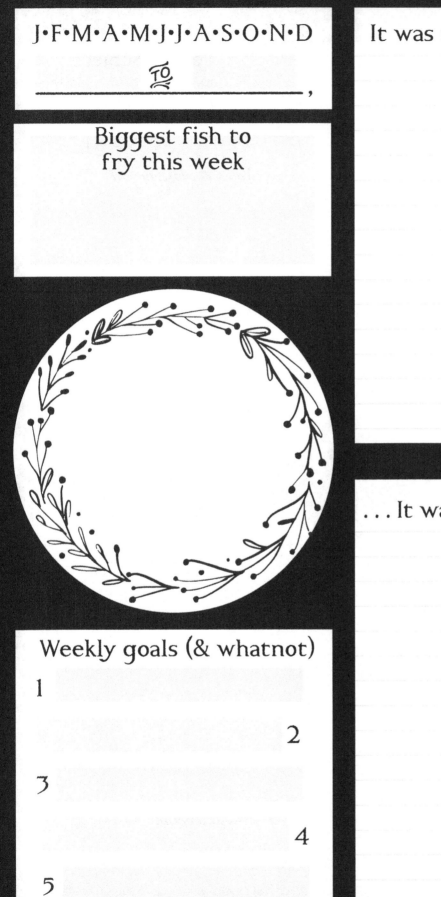

Weekly goals (& whatnot)

1

        2

3

        4

5

It was the best of times . . .

. . . It was the worst of times

Parent check~in
(How is your plague?)

	The rash is gone!	Slightly flushed	A few pustules	Throw me on the cart
S	○	○	○	○
M	○	○	○	○
T	○	○	○	○
W	○	○	○	○
T	○	○	○	○
F	○	○	○	○
S	○	○	○	○

Student check~in
(How are the humours?)

	Sprightly!	Fair	A bit lethargic	The bile is black
S	○	○	○	○
M	○	○	○	○
T	○	○	○	○
W	○	○	○	○
T	○	○	○	○
F	○	○	○	○
S	○	○	○	○

Tolling of the bell
(School day routine)

Time	Activity	M	T	W	T	F
		☐	☐	☐	☐	☐
		☐	☐	☐	☐	☐
		☐	☐	☐	☐	☐
		☐	☐	☐	☐	☐
		☐	☐	☐	☐	☐
		☐	☐	☐	☐	☐
		☐	☐	☐	☐	☐
		☐	☐	☐	☐	☐
		☐	☐	☐	☐	☐
		☐	☐	☐	☐	☐
		☐	☐	☐	☐	☐
		☐	☐	☐	☐	☐
		☐	☐	☐	☐	☐
		☐	☐	☐	☐	☐
		☐	☐	☐	☐	☐
		☐	☐	☐	☐	☐
		☐	☐	☐	☐	☐

Saturday	Sunday

Bird's~eye view of the week
(A glimpse from the top of the tower)

Monday	Tuesday	Wednesday	Thursday	Friday

Weekly Class Notes

Period/Subject

Teacher Check-in
M T W T F
○ ○ ○ ○ ○

Class Attendance
M T W T F
○ ○ ○ ○ ○ in person
○ ○ ○ ○ ○ online

Notes & Assignments

— Important —

Period/Subject

Teacher Check-in
M T W T F
○ ○ ○ ○ ○

Class Attendance
M T W T F
○ ○ ○ ○ ○ in person
○ ○ ○ ○ ○ online

Notes & Assignments

— Important —

Screen Breaks
— *Morning* —
Fresh Air

Period/Subject

Teacher Check-in
M T W T F
○ ○ ○ ○ ○

Class Attendance
M T W T F
○ ○ ○ ○ ○ in person
○ ○ ○ ○ ○ online

Notes & Assignments

— Important —

Period/Subject

Teacher Check-in
M T W T F
○ ○ ○ ○ ○

Class Attendance
M T W T F
○ ○ ○ ○ ○ in person
○ ○ ○ ○ ○ online

Notes & Assignments

— Important —

Weekly Class Notes

Period/Subject

Teacher Check-in
M T W T F
○ ○ ○ ○ ○

Class Attendance
M T W T F
○ ○ ○ ○ ○ *in person*
○ ○ ○ ○ ○ *online*

Notes & Assignments

— Important —

Period/Subject

Teacher Check-in
M T W T F
○ ○ ○ ○ ○

Class Attendance
M T W T F
○ ○ ○ ○ ○ *in person*
○ ○ ○ ○ ○ *online*

Notes & Assignments

— Important —

Screen Breaks
Afternoon
M T W T F
● ● ● ● ●
Fresh Air
M T W T F
● ● ● ● ●

Period/Subject

Teacher Check-in
M T W T F
○ ○ ○ ○ ○

Class Attendance
M T W T F
○ ○ ○ ○ ○ *in person*
○ ○ ○ ○ ○ *online*

Notes & Assignments

— Important —

Period/Subject

Teacher Check-in
M T W T F
○ ○ ○ ○ ○

Class Attendance
M T W T F
○ ○ ○ ○ ○ *in person*
○ ○ ○ ○ ○ *online*

Notes & Assignments

— Important —

J·F·M·A·M·J·J·A·S·O·N·D

_____ TO _____ ,

Biggest fish to fry this week

Weekly goals (& whatnot)

1

2

3

4

5

It was the best of times . . .

. . . It was the worst of times

Parent check~in
(How is your plague?)

	The rash is gone!	Slightly flushed	A few pustules	Throw me on the cart
S	○	○	○	○
M	○	○	○	○
T	○	○	○	○
W	○	○	○	○
T	○	○	○	○
F	○	○	○	○
S	○	○	○	○

Student check~in
(How are the humours?)

	Sprightly!	Fair	A bit lethargic	The bile is black
S	○	○	○	○
M	○	○	○	○
T	○	○	○	○
W	○	○	○	○
T	○	○	○	○
F	○	○	○	○
S	○	○	○	○

Tolling of the bell
(School day routine)

Time	Activity	M	T	W	T	F
		☐	☐	☐	☐	☐
		☐	☐	☐	☐	☐
		☐	☐	☐	☐	☐
		☐	☐	☐	☐	☐
		☐	☐	☐	☐	☐
		☐	☐	☐	☐	☐
		☐	☐	☐	☐	☐
		☐	☐	☐	☐	☐
		☐	☐	☐	☐	☐
		☐	☐	☐	☐	☐
		☐	☐	☐	☐	☐
		☐	☐	☐	☐	☐
		☐	☐	☐	☐	☐
		☐	☐	☐	☐	☐
		☐	☐	☐	☐	☐

Saturday	Sunday

Bird's~eye view of the week
(A glimpse from the top of the tower)

Monday	Tuesday	Wednesday	Thursday	Friday

Weekly Class Notes

Period/Subject

Teacher Check-in
M T W T F
○ ○ ○ ○ ○

Class Attendance
M T W T F
○ ○ ○ ○ ○ in person
○ ○ ○ ○ ○ online

Notes & Assignments

☐
☐
☐
☐
☐
☐
☐

— Important —

Period/Subject

Teacher Check-in
M T W T F
○ ○ ○ ○ ○

Class Attendance
M T W T F
○ ○ ○ ○ ○ in person
○ ○ ○ ○ ○ online

Notes & Assignments

☐
☐
☐
☐
☐

— Important —

Screen Breaks
— *Morning* —
Fresh Air

Period/Subject

Teacher Check-in
M T W T F
○ ○ ○ ○ ○

Class Attendance
M T W T F
○ ○ ○ ○ ○ in person
○ ○ ○ ○ ○ online

Notes & Assignments

☐
☐
☐
☐
☐

— Important —

Period/Subject

Teacher Check-in
M T W T F
○ ○ ○ ○ ○

Class Attendance
M T W T F
○ ○ ○ ○ ○ in person
○ ○ ○ ○ ○ online

Notes & Assignments

☐
☐
☐
☐
☐

— Important —

Weekly Class Notes

Period/Subject

Teacher Check-in
M T W T F
○ ○ ○ ○ ○

Class Attendance
M T W T F
○ ○ ○ ○ ○ *in person*
○ ○ ○ ○ ○ *online*

Notes & Assignments

☐
☐
☐
☐
☐
☐
☐

— *Important* —

Period/Subject

Teacher Check-in
M T W T F
○ ○ ○ ○ ○

Class Attendance
M T W T F
○ ○ ○ ○ ○ *in person*
○ ○ ○ ○ ○ *online*

Notes & Assignments

☐
☐
☐
☐
☐
☐
☐

— *Important* —

M T W T F
● ● ● ● ●
Screen Breaks
Afternoon
Fresh Air
M T W T F
● ● ● ● ●

Period/Subject

Teacher Check-in
M T W T F
○ ○ ○ ○ ○

Class Attendance
M T W T F
○ ○ ○ ○ ○ *in person*
○ ○ ○ ○ ○ *online*

Notes & Assignments

☐
☐
☐
☐
☐
☐
☐

— *Important* —

Period/Subject

Teacher Check-in
M T W T F
○ ○ ○ ○ ○

Class Attendance
M T W T F
○ ○ ○ ○ ○ *in person*
○ ○ ○ ○ ○ *online*

Notes & Assignments

☐
☐
☐
☐
☐
☐
☐

— *Important* —

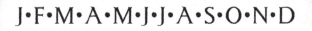

_____ TO _____ ,

Biggest fish to
fry this week

It was the best of times . . .

. . . It was the worst of times

Weekly goals (& whatnot)

1

           2

3

           4

5

Parent check~in
(How is your plague?)

	The rash is gone!	Slightly flushed	A few pustules	Throw me on the cart
S	○	○	○	○
M	○	○	○	○
T	○	○	○	○
W	○	○	○	○
T	○	○	○	○
F	○	○	○	○
S	○	○	○	○

Student check~in
(How are the humours?)

	Sprightly!	Fair	A bit lethargic	The bile is black
S	○	○	○	○
M	○	○	○	○
T	○	○	○	○
W	○	○	○	○
T	○	○	○	○
F	○	○	○	○
S	○	○	○	○

Tolling of the bell
(School day routine)

Time	Activity	M	T	W	T	F

Saturday	Sunday

Bird's~eye view of the week
(A glimpse from the top of the tower)

Monday	Tuesday	Wednesday	Thursday	Friday

Weekly Class Notes

Period/Subject

Teacher Check-in
M T W T F
○ ○ ○ ○ ○

Class Attendance
M T W T F
○ ○ ○ ○ ○ — *in person*
○ ○ ○ ○ ○ — *online*

Notes & Assignments

☐
☐
☐
☐
☐
☐
☐

— *Important* —

Period/Subject

Teacher Check-in
M T W T F
○ ○ ○ ○ ○

Class Attendance
M T W T F
○ ○ ○ ○ ○ — *in person*
○ ○ ○ ○ ○ — *online*

Notes & Assignments

☐
☐
☐
☐
☐
☐
☐

— *Important* —

Screen Breaks
— *Morning* —
Fresh Air

Period/Subject

Teacher Check-in
M T W T F
○ ○ ○ ○ ○

Class Attendance
M T W T F
○ ○ ○ ○ ○ — *in person*
○ ○ ○ ○ ○ — *online*

Notes & Assignments

☐
☐
☐
☐
☐
☐

— *Important* —

Period/Subject

Teacher Check-in
M T W T F
○ ○ ○ ○ ○

Class Attendance
M T W T F
○ ○ ○ ○ ○ — *in person*
○ ○ ○ ○ ○ — *online*

Notes & Assignments

☐
☐
☐
☐
☐
☐

— *Important* —

Weekly Class Notes

Period/Subject

Teacher Check-in
M T W T F
○ ○ ○ ○ ○

Class Attendance
M T W T F
○ ○ ○ ○ ○ in person
○ ○ ○ ○ ○ online

Notes & Assignments

— Important —

Period/Subject

Teacher Check-in
M T W T F
○ ○ ○ ○ ○

Class Attendance
M T W T F
○ ○ ○ ○ ○ in person
○ ○ ○ ○ ○ online

Notes & Assignments

— Important —

Screen Breaks
— *Afternoon* —
Fresh Air

Period/Subject

Teacher Check-in
M T W T F
○ ○ ○ ○ ○

Class Attendance
M T W T F
○ ○ ○ ○ ○ in person
○ ○ ○ ○ ○ online

Notes & Assignments

— Important —

Period/Subject

Teacher Check-in
M T W T F
○ ○ ○ ○ ○

Class Attendance
M T W T F
○ ○ ○ ○ ○ in person
○ ○ ○ ○ ○ online

Notes & Assignments

— Important —

J·F·M·A·M·J·J·A·S·O·N·D

_____ TO _____ ,

Biggest fish to fry this week

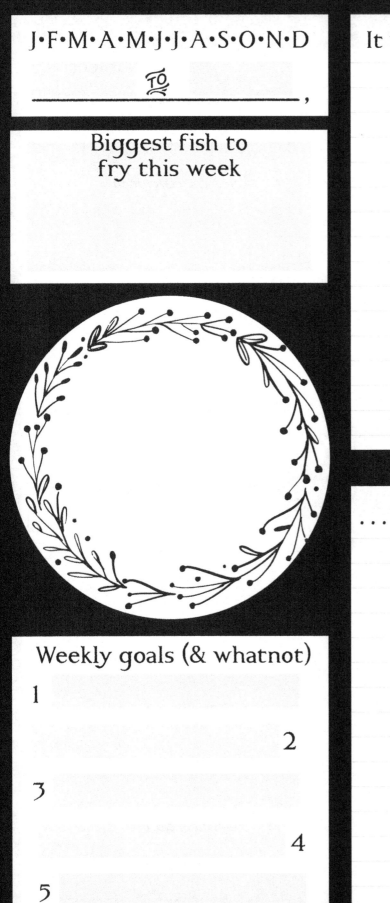

Weekly goals (& whatnot)

1

2

3

4

5

It was the best of times . . .

. . . It was the worst of times

Parent check~in
(How is your plague?)

	The rash is gone!	Slightly flushed	A few pustules	Throw me on the cart
S	○	○	○	○
M	○	○	○	○
T	○	○	○	○
W	○	○	○	○
T	○	○	○	○
F	○	○	○	○
S	○	○	○	○

Student check~in
(How are the humours?)

	Sprightly!	Fair	A bit lethargic	The bile is black
S	○	○	○	○
M	○	○	○	○
T	○	○	○	○
W	○	○	○	○
T	○	○	○	○
F	○	○	○	○
S	○	○	○	○

Tolling of the bell
(School day routine)

Time	Activity	M	T	W	T	F

Saturday	Sunday

Bird's~eye view of the week
(A glimpse from the top of the tower)

Monday	Tuesday	Wednesday	Thursday	Friday

Weekly Class Notes

Period/Subject

Teacher Check-in
M T W T F
○ ○ ○ ○ ○

Class Attendance
M T W T F
○ ○ ○ ○ ○ in person
○ ○ ○ ○ ○ online

Notes & Assignments

— Important —

Period/Subject

Teacher Check-in
M T W T F
○ ○ ○ ○ ○

Class Attendance
M T W T F
○ ○ ○ ○ ○ in person
○ ○ ○ ○ ○ online

Notes & Assignments

— Important —

Screen Breaks
— *Morning* —
Fresh Air

Period/Subject

Teacher Check-in
M T W T F
○ ○ ○ ○ ○

Class Attendance
M T W T F
○ ○ ○ ○ ○ in person
○ ○ ○ ○ ○ online

Notes & Assignments

— Important —

Period/Subject

Teacher Check-in
M T W T F
○ ○ ○ ○ ○

Class Attendance
M T W T F
○ ○ ○ ○ ○ in person
○ ○ ○ ○ ○ online

Notes & Assignments

— Important —

Weekly Class Notes

Period/Subject

Teacher Check-in
M T W T F
○ ○ ○ ○ ○

Class Attendance
M T W T F
○ ○ ○ ○ ○ *in person*
○ ○ ○ ○ ○ *online*

Notes & Assignments

— *Important* —

Period/Subject

Teacher Check-in
M T W T F
○ ○ ○ ○ ○

Class Attendance
M T W T F
○ ○ ○ ○ ○ *in person*
○ ○ ○ ○ ○ *online*

Notes & Assignments

— *Important* —

Screen Breaks
Afternoon
M T W T F
● ● ● ● ●
Fresh Air
M T W T F
● ● ● ● ●

Period/Subject

Teacher Check-in
M T W T F
○ ○ ○ ○ ○

Class Attendance
M T W T F
○ ○ ○ ○ ○ *in person*
○ ○ ○ ○ ○ *online*

Notes & Assignments

— *Important* —

Period/Subject

Teacher Check-in
M T W T F
○ ○ ○ ○ ○

Class Attendance
M T W T F
○ ○ ○ ○ ○ *in person*
○ ○ ○ ○ ○ *online*

Notes & Assignments

— *Important* —

J·F·M·A·M·J·J·A·S·O·N·D

TO

_____ ,

Biggest fish to
fry this week

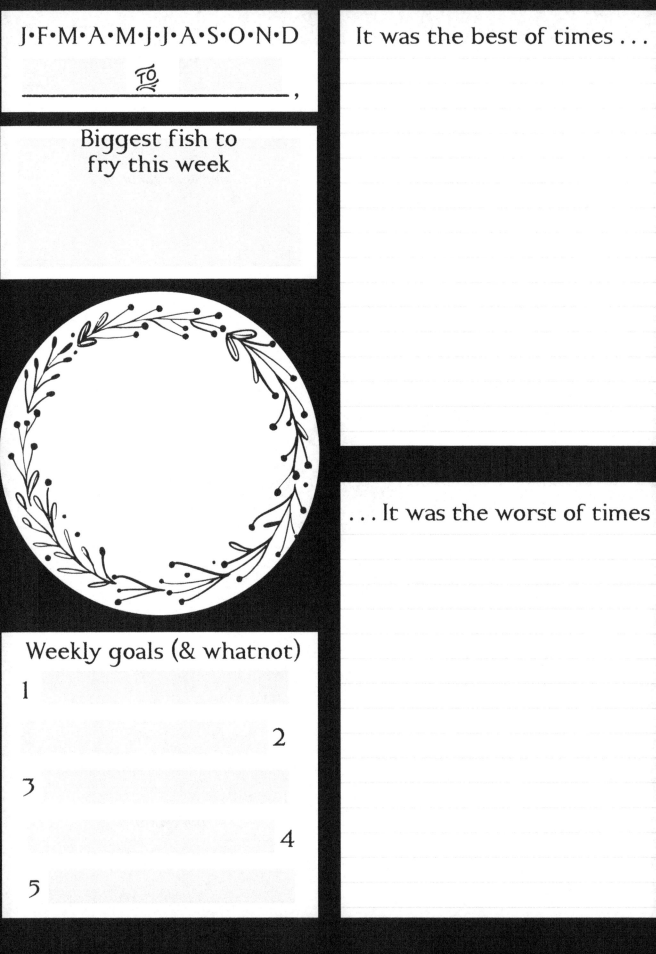

It was the best of times . . .

. . . It was the worst of times

Weekly goals (& whatnot)

1

2

3

4

5

Parent check~in
(How is your plague?)

	The rash is gone!	Slightly flushed	A few pustules	Throw me on the cart
S	○	○	○	○
M	○	○	○	○
T	○	○	○	○
W	○	○	○	○
T	○	○	○	○
F	○	○	○	○
S	○	○	○	○

Student check~in
(How are the humours?)

	Sprightly!	Fair	A bit lethargic	The bile is black
S	○	○	○	○
M	○	○	○	○
T	○	○	○	○
W	○	○	○	○
T	○	○	○	○
F	○	○	○	○
S	○	○	○	○

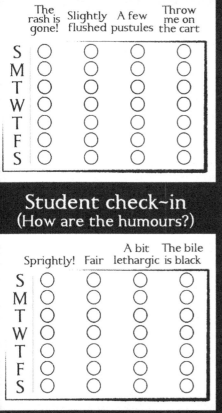

Tolling of the bell
(School day routine)

Time	*Activity*	M	T	W	T	F

Saturday	Sunday

Bird's~eye view of the week
(A glimpse from the top of the tower)

Monday	Tuesday	Wednesday	Thursday	Friday

Weekly Class Notes

Period/Subject

Teacher Check-in
M T W T F
○ ○ ○ ○ ○

Class Attendance
M T W T F
○ ○ ○ ○ ○ *in person*
○ ○ ○ ○ ○ *online*

Notes & Assignments

— Important —

Period/Subject

Teacher Check-in
M T W T F
○ ○ ○ ○ ○

Class Attendance
M T W T F
○ ○ ○ ○ ○ *in person*
○ ○ ○ ○ ○ *online*

Notes & Assignments

— Important —

Screen Breaks
— *Morning* —
Fresh Air

M W T F
M T W

Period/Subject

Teacher Check-in
M T W T F
○ ○ ○ ○ ○

Class Attendance
M T W T F
○ ○ ○ ○ ○ *in person*
○ ○ ○ ○ ○ *online*

Notes & Assignments

— Important —

Period/Subject

Teacher Check-in
M T W T F
○ ○ ○ ○ ○

Class Attendance
M T W T F
○ ○ ○ ○ ○ *in person*
○ ○ ○ ○ ○ *online*

Notes & Assignments

— Important —

Weekly Class Notes

Period/Subject

Teacher Check-in
M T W T F
○ ○ ○ ○ ○

Class Attendance
M T W T F
○ ○ ○ ○ ○ *in person*
○ ○ ○ ○ ○ *online*

Notes & Assignments

— Important —

Period/Subject

Teacher Check-in
M T W T F
○ ○ ○ ○ ○

Class Attendance
M T W T F
○ ○ ○ ○ ○ *in person*
○ ○ ○ ○ ○ *online*

Notes & Assignments

— Important —

Screen Breaks
Afternoon
Fresh Air

M T W T F

Period/Subject

Teacher Check-in
M T W T F
○ ○ ○ ○ ○

Class Attendance
M T W T F
○ ○ ○ ○ ○ *in person*
○ ○ ○ ○ ○ *online*

Notes & Assignments

— Important —

Period/Subject

Teacher Check-in
M T W T F
○ ○ ○ ○ ○

Class Attendance
M T W T F
○ ○ ○ ○ ○ *in person*
○ ○ ○ ○ ○ *online*

Notes & Assignments

— Important —

J·F·M·A·M·J·J·A·S·O·N·D

_TO_

_____ ,

Biggest fish to
fry this week

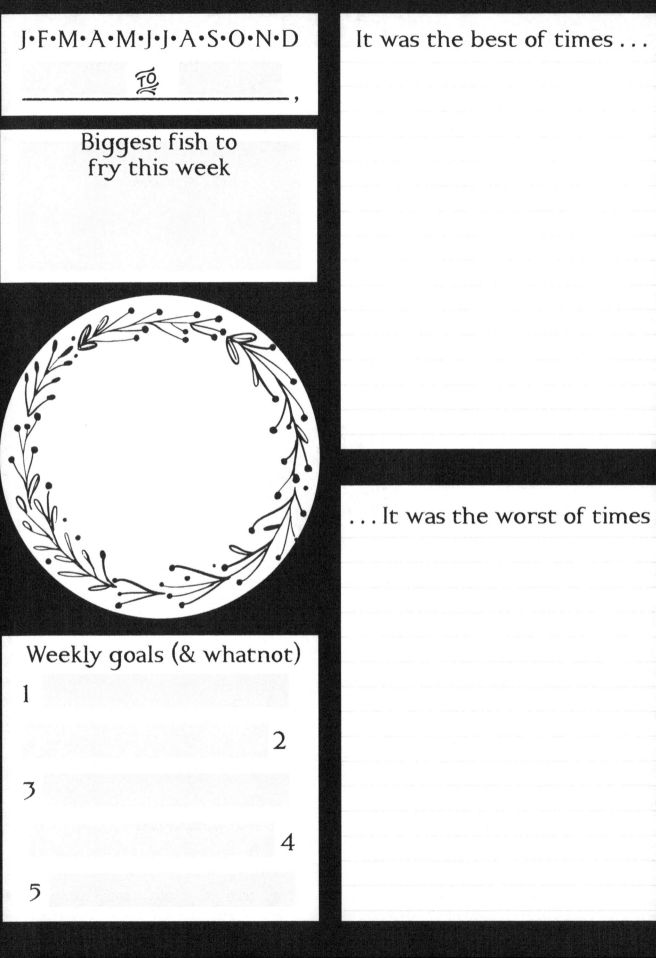

Weekly goals (& whatnot)

1

2

3

4

5

It was the best of times . . .

. . . It was the worst of times

Parent check~in
(How is your plague?)

	The rash is gone!	Slightly flushed	A few pustules	Throw me on the cart
S	○	○	○	○
M	○	○	○	○
T	○	○	○	○
W	○	○	○	○
T	○	○	○	○
F	○	○	○	○
S	○	○	○	○

Student check~in
(How are the humours?)

	Sprightly!	Fair	A bit lethargic	The bile is black
S	○	○	○	○
M	○	○	○	○
T	○	○	○	○
W	○	○	○	○
T	○	○	○	○
F	○	○	○	○
S	○	○	○	○

Tolling of the bell
(School day routine)

Time	Activity	M	T	W	T	F
		☐	☐	☐	☐	☐
		☐	☐	☐	☐	☐
		☐	☐	☐	☐	☐
		☐	☐	☐	☐	☐
		☐	☐	☐	☐	☐
		☐	☐	☐	☐	☐
		☐	☐	☐	☐	☐
		☐	☐	☐	☐	☐
		☐	☐	☐	☐	☐
		☐	☐	☐	☐	☐
		☐	☐	☐	☐	☐
		☐	☐	☐	☐	☐
		☐	☐	☐	☐	☐
		☐	☐	☐	☐	☐
		☐	☐	☐	☐	☐
		☐	☐	☐	☐	☐
		☐	☐	☐	☐	☐
		☐	☐	☐	☐	☐

Saturday	Sunday

Bird's~eye view of the week
(A glimpse from the top of the tower)

Monday	Tuesday	Wednesday	Thursday	Friday

Weekly Class Notes

Period/Subject

Teacher Check-in
M T W T F
○ ○ ○ ○ ○

Class Attendance
M T W T F
○ ○ ○ ○ ○ in person
○ ○ ○ ○ ○ online

Notes & Assignments

— *Important* —

Period/Subject

Teacher Check-in
M T W T F
○ ○ ○ ○ ○

Class Attendance
M T W T F
○ ○ ○ ○ ○ in person
○ ○ ○ ○ ○ online

Notes & Assignments

— *Important* —

Screen Breaks
— *Morning* —
Fresh Air

Period/Subject

Teacher Check-in
M T W T F
○ ○ ○ ○ ○

Class Attendance
M T W T F
○ ○ ○ ○ ○ in person
○ ○ ○ ○ ○ online

Notes & Assignments

— *Important* —

Period/Subject

Teacher Check-in
M T W T F
○ ○ ○ ○ ○

Class Attendance
M T W T F
○ ○ ○ ○ ○ in person
○ ○ ○ ○ ○ online

Notes & Assignments

— *Important* —

Weekly Class Notes

Period/Subject

Teacher Check-in
M T W T F
○ ○ ○ ○ ○

Class Attendance
M T W T F
○ ○ ○ ○ ○ in person
○ ○ ○ ○ ○ online

Notes & Assignments

— Important —

Period/Subject

Teacher Check-in
M T W T F
○ ○ ○ ○ ○

Class Attendance
M T W T F
○ ○ ○ ○ ○ in person
○ ○ ○ ○ ○ online

Notes & Assignments

— Important —

Screen Breaks
Afternoon
Fresh Air

Period/Subject

Teacher Check-in
M T W T F
○ ○ ○ ○ ○

Class Attendance
M T W T F
○ ○ ○ ○ ○ in person
○ ○ ○ ○ ○ online

Notes & Assignments

— Important —

Period/Subject

Teacher Check-in
M T W T F
○ ○ ○ ○ ○

Class Attendance
M T W T F
○ ○ ○ ○ ○ in person
○ ○ ○ ○ ○ online

Notes & Assignments

— Important —

J·F·M·A·M·J·J·A·S·O·N·D

_TO_

_____ ,

It was the best of times . . .

Biggest fish to fry this week

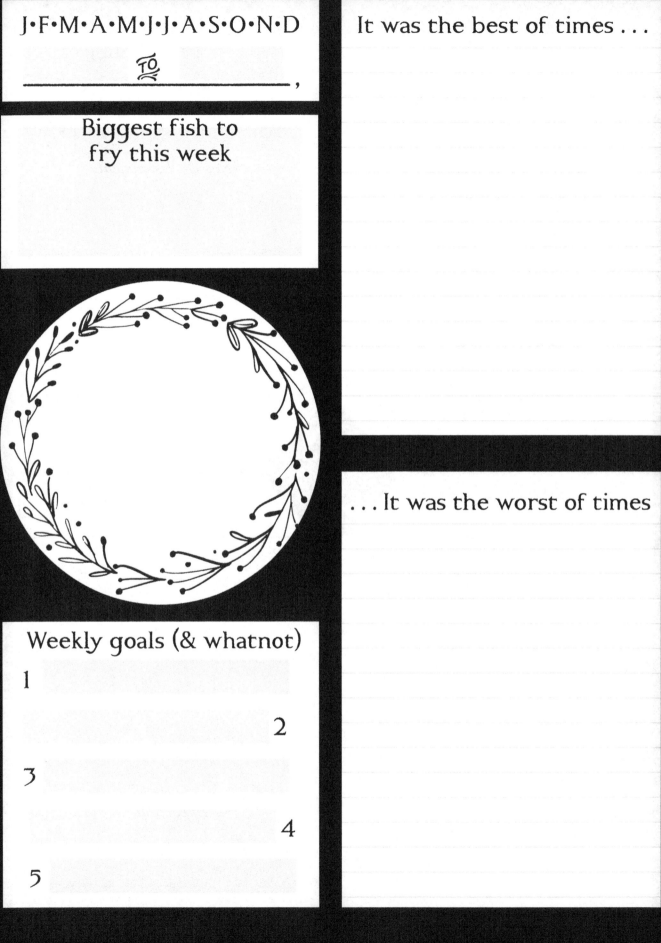

. . . It was the worst of times

Weekly goals (& whatnot)

1

2

3

4

5

Parent check~in
(How is your plague?)

	The rash is gone!	Slightly flushed	A few pustules	Throw me on the cart
S	○	○	○	○
M	○	○	○	○
T	○	○	○	○
W	○	○	○	○
T	○	○	○	○
F	○	○	○	○
S	○	○	○	○

Student check~in
(How are the humours?)

	Sprightly!	Fair	A bit lethargic	The bile is black
S	○	○	○	○
M	○	○	○	○
T	○	○	○	○
W	○	○	○	○
T	○	○	○	○
F	○	○	○	○
S	○	○	○	○

Tolling of the bell
(School day routine)

Time	Activity	M	T	W	T	F
		☐	☐	☐	☐	☐
		☐	☐	☐	☐	☐
		☐	☐	☐	☐	☐
		☐	☐	☐	☐	☐
		☐	☐	☐	☐	☐
		☐	☐	☐	☐	☐
		☐	☐	☐	☐	☐
		☐	☐	☐	☐	☐
		☐	☐	☐	☐	☐
		☐	☐	☐	☐	☐
		☐	☐	☐	☐	☐
		☐	☐	☐	☐	☐
		☐	☐	☐	☐	☐
		☐	☐	☐	☐	☐
		☐	☐	☐	☐	☐
		☐	☐	☐	☐	☐
		☐	☐	☐	☐	☐
		☐	☐	☐	☐	☐

Saturday	Sunday

Bird's~eye view of the week
(A glimpse from the top of the tower)

Monday	Tuesday	Wednesday	Thursday	Friday

Weekly Class Notes

Period/Subject

Teacher Check-in
M T W T F
○ ○ ○ ○ ○

Class Attendance
M T W T F
○ ○ ○ ○ ○ — in person
○ ○ ○ ○ ○ — online

Notes & Assignments

☐
☐
☐
☐
☐
☐
☐

— Important —

Period/Subject

Teacher Check-in
M T W T F
○ ○ ○ ○ ○

Class Attendance
M T W T F
○ ○ ○ ○ ○ — in person
○ ○ ○ ○ ○ — online

Notes & Assignments

☐
☐
☐
☐
☐
☐
☐

— Important —

Screen Breaks
— Morning —
Fresh Air
M T W T F

Period/Subject

Teacher Check-in
M T W T F
○ ○ ○ ○ ○

Class Attendance
M T W T F
○ ○ ○ ○ ○ — in person
○ ○ ○ ○ ○ — online

Notes & Assignments

☐
☐
☐
☐
☐
☐
☐

— Important —

Period/Subject

Teacher Check-in
M T W T F
○ ○ ○ ○ ○

Class Attendance
M T W T F
○ ○ ○ ○ ○ — in person
○ ○ ○ ○ ○ — online

Notes & Assignments

☐
☐
☐
☐
☐
☐
☐

— Important —

Weekly Class Notes

Period/Subject

Teacher Check-in
M T W T F
○ ○ ○ ○ ○

Class Attendance
M T W T F
○ ○ ○ ○ ○ *in person*
○ ○ ○ ○ ○ *online*

Notes & Assignments

— *Important* —

Period/Subject

Teacher Check-in
M T W T F
○ ○ ○ ○ ○

Class Attendance
M T W T F
○ ○ ○ ○ ○ *in person*
○ ○ ○ ○ ○ *online*

Notes & Assignments

— *Important* —

Screen Breaks
Afternoon
Fresh Air

M T W T F

M T W F

Period/Subject

Teacher Check-in
M T W T F
○ ○ ○ ○ ○

Class Attendance
M T W T F
○ ○ ○ ○ ○ *in person*
○ ○ ○ ○ ○ *online*

Notes & Assignments

— *Important* —

Period/Subject

Teacher Check-in
M T W T F
○ ○ ○ ○ ○

Class Attendance
M T W T F
○ ○ ○ ○ ○ *in person*
○ ○ ○ ○ ○ *online*

Notes & Assignments

— *Important* —

J·F·M·A·M·J·J·A·S·O·N·D

_TO_

_____,

Biggest fish to fry this week

It was the best of times . . .

. . . It was the worst of times

Weekly goals (& whatnot)

1

2

3

4

5

Parent check~in
(How is your plague?)

	The rash is gone!	Slightly flushed	A few pustules	Throw me on the cart
S	○	○	○	○
M	○	○	○	○
T	○	○	○	○
W	○	○	○	○
T	○	○	○	○
F	○	○	○	○
S	○	○	○	○

Student check~in
(How are the humours?)

	Sprightly!	Fair	A bit lethargic	The bile is black
S	○	○	○	○
M	○	○	○	○
T	○	○	○	○
W	○	○	○	○
T	○	○	○	○
F	○	○	○	○
S	○	○	○	○

Tolling of the bell
(School day routine)

Time	*Activity*	M	T	W	T	F

Saturday	Sunday

Bird's~eye view of the week
(A glimpse from the top of the tower)

Monday	Tuesday	Wednesday	Thursday	Friday

Weekly Class Notes

Period/Subject

Teacher Check-in
M T W T F
○ ○ ○ ○ ○

Class Attendance
M T W T F
○ ○ ○ ○ ○ *in person*
○ ○ ○ ○ ○ *online*

Notes & Assignments

☐
☐
☐
☐
☐
☐

— Important —

Period/Subject

Teacher Check-in
M T W T F
○ ○ ○ ○ ○

Class Attendance
M T W T F
○ ○ ○ ○ ○ *in person*
○ ○ ○ ○ ○ *online*

Notes & Assignments

☐
☐
☐
☐
☐
☐

— Important —

Screen Breaks
— Morning —
Fresh Air

M T W T F
M T W T F

Period/Subject

Teacher Check-in
M T W T F
○ ○ ○ ○ ○

Class Attendance
M T W T F
○ ○ ○ ○ ○ *in person*
○ ○ ○ ○ ○ *online*

Notes & Assignments

☐
☐
☐
☐
☐
☐

— Important —

Period/Subject

Teacher Check-in
M T W T F
○ ○ ○ ○ ○

Class Attendance
M T W T F
○ ○ ○ ○ ○ *in person*
○ ○ ○ ○ ○ *online*

Notes & Assignments

☐
☐
☐
☐
☐
☐

— Important —

Weekly Class Notes

Period/Subject

Teacher Check-in
M T W T F
○ ○ ○ ○ ○

Class Attendance
M T W T F
○ ○ ○ ○ ○ in person
○ ○ ○ ○ ○ online

Notes & Assignments

— Important —

Period/Subject

Teacher Check-in
M T W T F
○ ○ ○ ○ ○

Class Attendance
M T W T F
○ ○ ○ ○ ○ in person
○ ○ ○ ○ ○ online

Notes & Assignments

— Important —

Screen Breaks
M T W T F
Afternoon
Fresh Air
M T W T F

Period/Subject

Teacher Check-in
M T W T F
○ ○ ○ ○ ○

Class Attendance
M T W T F
○ ○ ○ ○ ○ in person
○ ○ ○ ○ ○ online

Notes & Assignments

— Important —

Period/Subject

Teacher Check-in
M T W T F
○ ○ ○ ○ ○

Class Attendance
M T W T F
○ ○ ○ ○ ○ in person
○ ○ ○ ○ ○ online

Notes & Assignments

— Important —

J·F·M·A·M·J·J·A·S·O·N·D

_to_

_____,

Biggest fish to fry this week

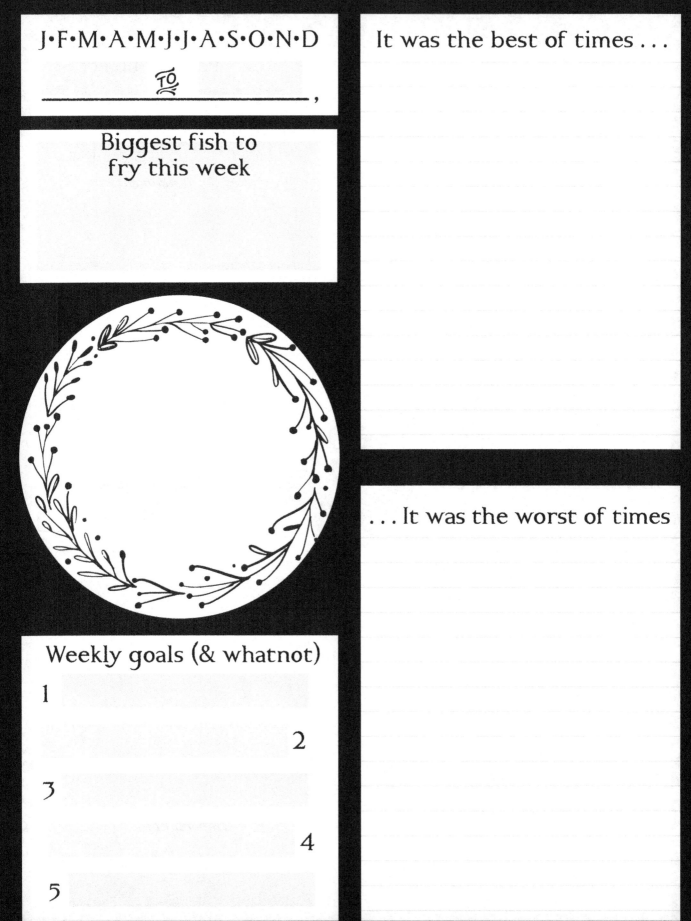

Weekly goals (& whatnot)

1

2

3

4

5

It was the best of times . . .

. . . It was the worst of times

Parent check~in
(How is your plague?)

	The rash is gone!	Slightly flushed	A few pustules	Throw me on the cart
S	○	○	○	○
M	○	○	○	○
T	○	○	○	○
W	○	○	○	○
T	○	○	○	○
F	○	○	○	○
S	○	○	○	○

Student check~in
(How are the humours?)

	Sprightly!	Fair	A bit lethargic	The bile is black
S	○	○	○	○
M	○	○	○	○
T	○	○	○	○
W	○	○	○	○
T	○	○	○	○
F	○	○	○	○
S	○	○	○	○

Tolling of the bell
(School day routine)

Time	Activity	M	T	W	T	F

Saturday	Sunday

Bird's~eye view of the week
(A glimpse from the top of the tower)

Monday	Tuesday	Wednesday	Thursday	Friday

Weekly Class Notes

Period/Subject

Teacher Check-in
M T W T F
○ ○ ○ ○ ○

Class Attendance
M T W T F
○ ○ ○ ○ ○ *in person*
○ ○ ○ ○ ○ *online*

Notes & Assignments

— *Important* —

Period/Subject

Teacher Check-in
M T W T F
○ ○ ○ ○ ○

Class Attendance
M T W T F
○ ○ ○ ○ ○ *in person*
○ ○ ○ ○ ○ *online*

Notes & Assignments

— *Important* —

Screen Breaks
— *Morning* —
Fresh Air

W
M T T F
M T W T F

Period/Subject

Teacher Check-in
M T W T F
○ ○ ○ ○ ○

Class Attendance
M T W T F
○ ○ ○ ○ ○ *in person*
○ ○ ○ ○ ○ *online*

Notes & Assignments

— *Important* —

Period/Subject

Teacher Check-in
M T W T F
○ ○ ○ ○ ○

Class Attendance
M T W T F
○ ○ ○ ○ ○ *in person*
○ ○ ○ ○ ○ *online*

Notes & Assignments

— *Important* —

Weekly Class Notes

Period/Subject

Teacher Check-in
M T W T F
○ ○ ○ ○ ○

Class Attendance
M T W T F
○ ○ ○ ○ ○ *in person*
○ ○ ○ ○ ○ *online*

Notes & Assignments

☐
☐
☐
☐
☐
☐
☐

— Important —

Period/Subject

Teacher Check-in
M T W T F
○ ○ ○ ○ ○

Class Attendance
M T W T F
○ ○ ○ ○ ○ *in person*
○ ○ ○ ○ ○ *online*

Notes & Assignments

☐
☐
☐
☐
☐
☐
☐

— Important —

Screen Breaks
Afternoon
Fresh Air
M T W T F

Period/Subject

Teacher Check-in
M T W T F
○ ○ ○ ○ ○

Class Attendance
M T W T F
○ ○ ○ ○ ○ *in person*
○ ○ ○ ○ ○ *online*

Notes & Assignments

☐
☐
☐
☐
☐
☐
☐

— Important —

Period/Subject

Teacher Check-in
M T W T F
○ ○ ○ ○ ○

Class Attendance
M T W T F
○ ○ ○ ○ ○ *in person*
○ ○ ○ ○ ○ *online*

Notes & Assignments

☐
☐
☐
☐
☐
☐
☐

— Important —

J·F·M·A·M·J·J·A·S·O·N·D

TO

_____ ,

Biggest fish to fry this week

Weekly goals (& whatnot)

1

2

3

4

5

It was the best of times . . .

. . . It was the worst of times

Parent check~in
(How is your plague?)

	The rash is gone!	Slightly flushed	A few pustules	Throw me on the cart
S	○	○	○	○
M	○	○	○	○
T	○	○	○	○
W	○	○	○	○
T	○	○	○	○
F	○	○	○	○
S	○	○	○	○

Student check~in
(How are the humours?)

	Sprightly!	Fair	A bit lethargic	The bile is black
S	○	○	○	○
M	○	○	○	○
T	○	○	○	○
W	○	○	○	○
T	○	○	○	○
F	○	○	○	○
S	○	○	○	○

Tolling of the bell
(School day routine)

Time	Activity	M	T	W	T	F

Saturday	Sunday

Bird's~eye view of the week
(A glimpse from the top of the tower)

Monday	Tuesday	Wednesday	Thursday	Friday

Weekly Class Notes

Period/Subject

Teacher Check-in
M T W T F
○ ○ ○ ○ ○

Class Attendance
M T W T F
○ ○ ○ ○ ○ *in person*
○ ○ ○ ○ ○ *online*

Notes & Assignments

— Important —

Period/Subject

Teacher Check-in
M T W T F
○ ○ ○ ○ ○

Class Attendance
M T W T F
○ ○ ○ ○ ○ *in person*
○ ○ ○ ○ ○ *online*

Notes & Assignments

— Important —

Screen Breaks
Morning
Fresh Air

Period/Subject

Teacher Check-in
M T W T F
○ ○ ○ ○ ○

Class Attendance
M T W T F
○ ○ ○ ○ ○ *in person*
○ ○ ○ ○ ○ *online*

Notes & Assignments

— Important —

Period/Subject

Teacher Check-in
M T W T F
○ ○ ○ ○ ○

Class Attendance
M T W T F
○ ○ ○ ○ ○ *in person*
○ ○ ○ ○ ○ *online*

Notes & Assignments

— Important —

Weekly Class Notes

Period/Subject

Teacher Check-in
M T W T F
○ ○ ○ ○ ○

Class Attendance
M T W T F
○ ○ ○ ○ ○ in person
○ ○ ○ ○ ○ online

Notes & Assignments

☐
☐
☐
☐
☐
☐
☐

— Important —

Period/Subject

Teacher Check-in
M T W T F
○ ○ ○ ○ ○

Class Attendance
M T W T F
○ ○ ○ ○ ○ in person
○ ○ ○ ○ ○ online

Notes & Assignments

☐
☐
☐
☐
☐
☐
☐

— Important —

Screen Breaks
M T W T F
○ ○ ○ ○ ○

Afternoon

Fresh Air
M T W T F
○ ○ ○ ○ ○

Period/Subject

Teacher Check-in
M T W T F
○ ○ ○ ○ ○

Class Attendance
M T W T F
○ ○ ○ ○ ○ in person
○ ○ ○ ○ ○ online

Notes & Assignments

☐
☐
☐
☐
☐
☐
☐

— Important —

Period/Subject

Teacher Check-in
M T W T F
○ ○ ○ ○ ○

Class Attendance
M T W T F
○ ○ ○ ○ ○ in person
○ ○ ○ ○ ○ online

Notes & Assignments

☐
☐
☐
☐
☐
☐
☐

— Important —

J·F·M·A·M·J·J·A·S·O·N·D

 TO

_____ ,

Biggest fish to fry this week

It was the best of times . . .

. . . It was the worst of times

Weekly goals (& whatnot)

1

2

3

4

5

Parent check~in
(How is your plague?)

	The rash is gone!	Slightly flushed	A few pustules	Throw me on the cart
S	○	○	○	○
M	○	○	○	○
T	○	○	○	○
W	○	○	○	○
T	○	○	○	○
F	○	○	○	○
S	○	○	○	○

Student check~in
(How are the humours?)

	Sprightly!	Fair	A bit lethargic	The bile is black
S	○	○	○	○
M	○	○	○	○
T	○	○	○	○
W	○	○	○	○
T	○	○	○	○
F	○	○	○	○
S	○	○	○	○

Tolling of the bell
(School day routine)

Time	*Activity*	M	T	W	T	F
		☐	☐	☐	☐	☐
		☐	☐	☐	☐	☐
		☐	☐	☐	☐	☐
		☐	☐	☐	☐	☐
		☐	☐	☐	☐	☐
		☐	☐	☐	☐	☐
		☐	☐	☐	☐	☐
		☐	☐	☐	☐	☐
		☐	☐	☐	☐	☐
		☐	☐	☐	☐	☐
		☐	☐	☐	☐	☐
		☐	☐	☐	☐	☐
		☐	☐	☐	☐	☐
		☐	☐	☐	☐	☐
		☐	☐	☐	☐	☐
		☐	☐	☐	☐	☐
		☐	☐	☐	☐	☐
		☐	☐	☐	☐	☐

Saturday	Sunday

Bird's~eye view of the week
(A glimpse from the top of the tower)

Monday	Tuesday	Wednesday	Thursday	Friday

Weekly Class Notes

Period/Subject

Teacher Check-in
M T W T F
○ ○ ○ ○ ○

Class Attendance
M T W T F
○ ○ ○ ○ ○ *in person*
○ ○ ○ ○ ○ *online*

Notes & Assignments

— Important —

Period/Subject

Teacher Check-in
M T W T F
○ ○ ○ ○ ○

Class Attendance
M T W T F
○ ○ ○ ○ ○ *in person*
○ ○ ○ ○ ○ *online*

Notes & Assignments

— Important —

Screen Breaks
— *Morning* —
Fresh Air

Period/Subject

Teacher Check-in
M T W T F
○ ○ ○ ○ ○

Class Attendance
M T W T F
○ ○ ○ ○ ○ *in person*
○ ○ ○ ○ ○ *online*

Notes & Assignments

— Important —

Period/Subject

Teacher Check-in
M T W T F
○ ○ ○ ○ ○

Class Attendance
M T W T F
○ ○ ○ ○ ○ *in person*
○ ○ ○ ○ ○ *online*

Notes & Assignments

— Important —

Weekly Class Notes

Period/Subject

Teacher Check-in
M T W T F
○ ○ ○ ○ ○

Class Attendance
M T W T F
○ ○ ○ ○ ○ *in person*
○ ○ ○ ○ ○ *online*

Notes & Assignments

— *Important* —

Period/Subject

Teacher Check-in
M T W T F
○ ○ ○ ○ ○

Class Attendance
M T W T F
○ ○ ○ ○ ○ *in person*
○ ○ ○ ○ ○ *online*

Notes & Assignments

— *Important* —

Screen Breaks
— *Afternoon* —
Fresh Air

Period/Subject

Teacher Check-in
M T W T F
○ ○ ○ ○ ○

Class Attendance
M T W T F
○ ○ ○ ○ ○ *in person*
○ ○ ○ ○ ○ *online*

Notes & Assignments

— *Important* —

Period/Subject

Teacher Check-in
M T W T F
○ ○ ○ ○ ○

Class Attendance
M T W T F
○ ○ ○ ○ ○ *in person*
○ ○ ○ ○ ○ *online*

Notes & Assignments

— *Important* —

J·F·M·A·M·J·J·A·S·O·N·D

_TO_

_____ ,

Biggest fish to fry this week

Weekly goals (& whatnot)

1

2

3

4

5

It was the best of times . . .

. . . It was the worst of times

Parent check~in
(How is your plague?)

	The rash is gone!	Slightly flushed	A few pustules	Throw me on the cart
S	○	○	○	○
M	○	○	○	○
T	○	○	○	○
W	○	○	○	○
T	○	○	○	○
F	○	○	○	○
S	○	○	○	○

Student check~in
(How are the humours?)

	Sprightly!	Fair	A bit lethargic	The bile is black
S	○	○	○	○
M	○	○	○	○
T	○	○	○	○
W	○	○	○	○
T	○	○	○	○
F	○	○	○	○
S	○	○	○	○

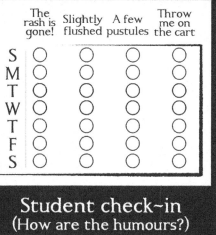

Tolling of the bell
(School day routine)

Time	Activity	M	T	W	T	F
		☐	☐	☐	☐	☐
		☐	☐	☐	☐	☐
		☐	☐	☐	☐	☐
		☐	☐	☐	☐	☐
		☐	☐	☐	☐	☐
		☐	☐	☐	☐	☐
		☐	☐	☐	☐	☐
		☐	☐	☐	☐	☐
		☐	☐	☐	☐	☐
		☐	☐	☐	☐	☐
		☐	☐	☐	☐	☐
		☐	☐	☐	☐	☐
		☐	☐	☐	☐	☐
		☐	☐	☐	☐	☐
		☐	☐	☐	☐	☐
		☐	☐	☐	☐	☐
		☐	☐	☐	☐	☐
		☐	☐	☐	☐	☐

Saturday	Sunday

Bird's~eye view of the week
(A glimpse from the top of the tower)

Monday	Tuesday	Wednesday	Thursday	Friday

Weekly Class Notes

Period/Subject

Teacher Check-in
M T W T F
○ ○ ○ ○ ○

Class Attendance
M T W T F
○ ○ ○ ○ ○ *in person*
○ ○ ○ ○ ○ *online*

Notes & Assignments

— *Important* —

Period/Subject

Teacher Check-in
M T W T F
○ ○ ○ ○ ○

Class Attendance
M T W T F
○ ○ ○ ○ ○ *in person*
○ ○ ○ ○ ○ *online*

Notes & Assignments

— *Important* —

Screen Breaks
— *Morning* —
Fresh Air

Period/Subject

Teacher Check-in
M T W T F
○ ○ ○ ○ ○

Class Attendance
M T W T F
○ ○ ○ ○ ○ *in person*
○ ○ ○ ○ ○ *online*

Notes & Assignments

— *Important* —

Period/Subject

Teacher Check-in
M T W T F
○ ○ ○ ○ ○

Class Attendance
M T W T F
○ ○ ○ ○ ○ *in person*
○ ○ ○ ○ ○ *online*

Notes & Assignments

— *Important* —

Weekly Class Notes

Period/Subject

Teacher Check-in
M T W T F
○ ○ ○ ○ ○

Class Attendance
M T W T F
○ ○ ○ ○ ○   in person
○ ○ ○ ○ ○   online

Notes & Assignments

☐
☐
☐
☐
☐
☐
☐

— *Important* —

Period/Subject

Teacher Check-in
M T W T F
○ ○ ○ ○ ○

Class Attendance
M T W T F
○ ○ ○ ○ ○   in person
○ ○ ○ ○ ○   online

Notes & Assignments

☐
☐
☐
☐
☐
☐
☐

— *Important* —

Screen Breaks
Afternoon
Fresh Air

Period/Subject

Teacher Check-in
M T W T F
○ ○ ○ ○ ○

Class Attendance
M T W T F
○ ○ ○ ○ ○   in person
○ ○ ○ ○ ○   online

Notes & Assignments

☐
☐
☐
☐
☐
☐
☐

— *Important* —

Period/Subject

Teacher Check-in
M T W T F
○ ○ ○ ○ ○

Class Attendance
M T W T F
○ ○ ○ ○ ○   in person
○ ○ ○ ○ ○   online

Notes & Assignments

☐
☐
☐
☐
☐
☐
☐

— *Important* —

Content of an indeterminate nature.

THE EXTRA PAGES AT THE BACK

- EXPENSE LEDGER
- KEEPER OF THE KEYS (PASSWORDS)
- CONTACTS
- PAGE OF WAYWARD STICKY NOTES
- IDEAS FOR FUN AND FROLIC
- NOTES TO MY FUTURE SELF
- READING LIST
- PEN/MARKER TEST PAGE

Expense Ledger

Date	Description	Amount
		Total

Keeper of the keys

Description	Logon ID	Password

Contacts

Name	E-Mail	Phone

Contacts

Name	E-Mail	Phone

Page of wayward sticky notes

Page of wayward sticky notes

Ideas for fun and frolic

Note to my future self

Reading List

Title	Author	Date

PEN TEST PAGE
Test your media here (pens, pencils, paint, markers, etc.)

NOTE TO READERS

Lovely parents and *others-who-teach!* We hope this book, which we handcrafted from the finest artisanal words and graphics just for you, helps you plan and play this school year.

If you are one of the folks who likes to review books, we'd love it if you posted a review for it on your favorite book spot. If you aren't a reviewing type, fear not, we will cherish you regardless.

We'd also like to encourage you to sign up for our newsletter at www.subscribepage.com/u5l9j8. Feel free to send/share with us any of your fun planning entries and ideas (but don't post anything you don't want everyone to see, or which would offend small children and dogs). You can share with us on our Facebook page at www.facebook.com/bee.moon.75491, or via e-mail at beeandmoonbooks@gmail.com.

You might also wish to look at the original *Love in the Time of the Plague* Journal (ISBN 978-1-952737-15-2) which is now available.

Blessings of the plague doctor, and don't get on the cart!

Katie &

LK

ABOUT THE AUTHORS

KATIE MACALISTER

A *New York Times, USA Today, and Publishers Weekly* bestseller, Katie MacAlister has always loved reading. Growing up in a family where a weekly visit to the library was a given, Katie spent much of her time with her nose buried in a book. Two years after she started writing novels, Katie sold her first romantic comedy. More than sixty books later, her novels have been translated into numerous languages, been recorded as audiobooks, received several awards, and are regulars on the bestseller lists. Katie lives in the Pacific Northwest with two dogs, and can often be found lurking around online.

LARON GLOVER

A graphic design artist and owner of Ninth Moon, LLC, Laron has worked with authors and business owners for over thirteen years designing and creating various promotional materials. She has a passion for innovative products, and a great attention to detail and is known for running with scissors and refusing to stay within the lines. She lives in the Pacific Northwest with her husband and son, and a herd of wild rabbits in her back yard.